VOL. 9 IN THE SEANET SERIES

D1070177

# COMPLEXITIES OF MONEY AND MISSIONS IN ASIA

## PAUL H. DE NEUI, EDITOR

**WILLIAM CAREY**
LIBRARY

Complexities of Money and Missions in Asia
Copyright © 2012 by Paul De Neui

*All rights reserved.*

No part of this book may be reproduced or transmitted in any form or by any means—for example, electronic or mechanical, including photocopying and recording—without the prior written permission of the publisher, except brief quotations used in connection with reviews in magazines or newspapers.

Unless otherwise noted, Scripture is taken from the Holy Bible, Today's New International® Version TNIV®. Copyright © 2001, 2005 by International Bible Society®. Used by permission of International Bible Society®. All rights reserved worldwide.

Published by William Carey Library
1605 E. Elizabeth Street
Pasadena, CA 91104 | www.missionbooks.org

Brad Koenig, copyeditor
Hugh Pindur, graphic design
Rose Lee-Norman, indexer

William Carey Library is a ministry of the
U.S. Center for World Mission
Pasadena, CA | www.uscwm.org

Printed in the United States of America

16 15 14 13 12    5 4 3 2 1 BP1000

---

Library of Congress Cataloging-in-Publication Data

Complexities of money and missions in Asia / Paul H. De Neui, editor.
    p. cm. -- (SEANET series ; v. 9)
Proceedings of a SEANET conference held in 2011 in Chiang Mai, Thailand.
Includes bibliographical references and index.
ISBN 978-0-87808-038-0
1. Missions to Buddhists--Congresses. 2. Christianity and other
religions--Buddhism--Congresses. 3.
Buddhism--Relations--Christianity--Congresses. 4. Money--Religious
aspects--Christianity--Congresses. 5. Money--Religious
aspects--Buddhism--Congresses. I. De Neui, Paul H.
    BV2618.C68 2011
    266.0088'2943--dc23

                    2011046132

# CONTENTS

# INTRODUCTION

The American sage Benjamin Franklin once wrote, "Who is rich? He that is content. Who is that? Nobody." Perhaps it is this lack of contentment that has caused so many Westerners, including Christ followers, to exclude themselves from the category of the rich. The word of God came through the Apostle Paul, "Command those who are rich in this present world not to be arrogant" (1 Tim 6:17), and Christians in the West respond, "Surely, not I, Lord?" The knowledge that godliness with contentment is great gain sounds fine in the home culture where there are always those with much more with whom one can compare. But what happens when a missionary is suddenly thrust into a context where the standard of living is so divergent that she or he is now the object of envy? What actual message is communicated through the wordless witness of the Western Christian missionary lifestyle? Is attraction to so-called good news now so financially focused that other foundational issues become overshadowed? This issue becomes even more complicated when the missionary arrives clueless about personal privilege, ignorant of the envy of others, and carries the mistaken attitude that others think similarly. As Austin O'Malley once said, "God shows his contempt for wealth by the kind of person he selects to receive it."

Buddhist teachings affirm that slavish attachment to the material attractions of this temporal world only results in greater personal and corporate suffering. Christian Scripture teaches that some, "eager for money, have wandered from the faith and pierced themselves with many griefs" (1 Tim 6:10). Buddha said, "Health is the highest gain, Contentment is the greatest wealth. The trusty are the best kinsmen" (*Dhammapada*, v. 204). Christ taught, "Look at the birds of the air; they do not sow or reap or store away in barns, and yet your heavenly Father feeds them. Are you not much more valuable than they?" (Matt 6:26). In spite of good teachings, both religious groups struggle in the tension to possess enough of wealth to live well while remaining free from the temptation to be completely preoccupied by the desire for more. Far too few have dared to dialogue on this complex, and for many, highly personal topic.

SEANET (South, South-east and North Asia Network) proudly presents *Complexities of Money and Missions in Asia* to address this glaring gap in missiological thinking. Each chapter included here represents years of personal struggle with this issue from both Western and non-Western reflective practitioners. G. P. V. Somaratna opens the volume with a helpful historical perspective held by Buddhists towards use of Christian missionary funds in his native Sri Lanka. Senior missionary statesmen Alex Smith writes from many years of personal service in Thailand. A new contributor, Andrew Thomas, lives out the complexities of money and mission daily in his adopted new home of Cambodia. Two scholarly contributors share both personal and academic insights: Jonathan Bonk, a well-known writer on this topic, and Mary Lederleitner with a wide range of experience with mission and money in many countries of Asia. Paul De Neui opens up the dialogue with confession and an appeal to reconsider the patron-client relationship in a new light. Finally David Lim challenges the reader to recognize that God's movement in the world progresses often in spite of material means. Each chapter includes much for reflection and application for mission in Asia and elsewhere in the world.

All of these chapters were first presented as papers at the 2011 SEANET conference held in Chiang Mai, Thailand. SEANET serves as a networking forum where groups and individuals can meet to reflect, celebrate, and strategize together in partnership with what God has initiated around the world. Over 140 delegates representing sixteen countries participated in the forum, and their helpful comments were incorporated by each of these authors in these edited chapters.

Publication of these helpful articles would not be possible without the contributions of many dedicated individuals. Thanks must go first of all to my diligent assistant Melissa Millis for many hours of reading, reviewing, corresponding, and correcting details. SEANET is especially grateful to William Carey Library for their ongoing commitment to expand missiological understanding through the publication of these volumes. Special recognition goes to general manager Jeff Minard, senior editor Kelley K. Wolfe, copyeditor, Brad Koenig, and graphic designer Hugh Pindur. Thanks to the local printers who made delivery of this volume possible in non-Western countries. Much gratitude to those who hand carry these volumes to libraries, schools, and groups who are beyond the reach of electronic mailing capacities.

May the prayer of the writer of Proverbs 30 be our own as we seek to reflect God's purposes in service in the world.

Paul H. De Neui
August 2011

Two things I ask of you, LORD;
do not refuse me before I die:
Keep falsehood and lies far from me;
give me neither poverty nor riches,
but give me only my daily bread.
Otherwise, I may have too much and disown you
and say, "Who is the LORD?"
Or I may become poor and steal,
and so dishonor the name of my God.

Proverbs 30:7–9

# CONTRIBUTORS

**Jonathan J. Bonk** is from Canada. He was raised in Ethiopia by missionary parents and served there with his wife in famine relief from 1974 to 1976. He is a graduate of Trinity Evangelical Divinity School and the University of Aberdeen. For twenty years he served as professor of global Christian studies at Providence College and Theological Seminary in Canada. A Mennonite minister, he has served as president of both the American Society of Missiology and the Association of Professors of Mission and is currently president of the International Association for Mission Studies. Currently he serves as the executive director of the Overseas Ministries Study Center in New Haven, Connecticut, and editor of the *International Bulletin of Missionary Research*. He is the author of numerous articles and reviews, and has published five books and edited several others. He serves as regular visiting professor of missions and evangelism at Yale Divinity School and at the Presbyterian College and Theological Seminary in Seoul.

**Paul H. De Neui** is from the United States. He and his wife served in a number of roles as missionaries in Thailand from 1987 to 2005. During these years they were involved in a variety of business ventures, promoting community development and church planting primarily in the northeast, Lao-speaking region known as Isaan. De Neui is a graduate of Fuller Theological Seminary and an ordained minister with the Evangelical Covenant Church. He has edited or coedited the last five SEANET volumes and serves on the SEANET steering committee as organizer of the annual missiological forum. In addition he has published numerous articles on contextualization issues within Asia. Based in Chicago, Illinois, he serves as professor of intercultural studies at North Park Theological Seminary and travels extensively as a missiology professor and trainer.

**Mary T. Lederleitner** is from the United States. Before entering ministry she became a certified public accountant and served as a tax examiner for the US Internal Revenue Service. She holds a master's degree in intercultural studies from Wheaton College. For twelve years she served as the Asia area finance manager and head of international audit for Wycliffe International. She has traveled extensively overseas and has been called upon to assist a wide range of Christian nonprofit ministries and churches. She is pursuing a PhD at Trinity Evangelical Divinity

School in educational studies. Lederleitner is on a number of advisory boards and committees and is also an adjunct professor at Wheaton College and North Park Theological Seminary. She recently published *Cross-cultural Partnerships: Navigating the Complexities of Money and Mission* with InterVarsity Press.

**David S. Lim** is from the Philippines. He had previously served as academic dean at Asian Theological Seminary in the Philippines and Oxford Centre for Mission Studies in the UK. His PhD in theology (New Testament) was earned from Fuller Theological Seminary. He now serves as the president of the Asian School of Development and Cross-cultural Studies, and president of China Ministries International–Philippines that recruits Filipino missionaries for China. Lim is the author of several books and articles on non-Western missiology, theological contextualization, and transformational development.

**Alex G. Smith** was born and raised in Australia. He graduated from the International Institute of Christian Communication in Kenya and Prairie Bible College in Canada. He earned graduate degrees from Western Evangelical and Fuller Theological Seminary. He is a veteran missionary to Thailand and founder of the Thailand Church Growth Committee and cofounder of SEANET. He served as adjunct faculty at Multnomah University for eighteen years. Presently he is a minister-at-large for Overseas Missionary Fellowship International, under which he has served for forty-seven years. He has published numerous books and articles on ministry in the Buddhist world.

**G. P. V. Somaratna** is from Sri Lanka. He has a PhD in South Asian history from the University of London. He served as professor of modern history at the University of Colombo, Sri Lanka, and is now serving as senior research professor at Colombo Theological Seminary. He has published numerous articles and books on the history of Sri Lanka and the impact of Christianity upon Sri Lankan Buddhism. He is widely regarded as one of Sri Lanka's leading scholars on Ceylonese history.

**Andrew Thomas** is from South Africa. He has a diploma in secondary education at Edgewood College of Education. After compulsory military training, he began a teaching career. In 1994 Andrew felt called to the ministry and resigned from teaching. He then spent six years in self-supporting ministry and informal training. In 2001 he left for further studies at Christ for the Nations (Dallas, Texas), receiving a leadership certificate, advanced diploma in pastoral ministry, and advanced diploma in children's ministry. He subsequently returned to South Africa and became a teacher at the South African Christ for the Nations Bible School from July 2004 until December 2006. In December 2006 he relocated to Cambodia where he presently resides. Currently he teaches children's ministry to church planters and pastors under the auspices of the Bible League. He also regularly preaches in several local churches and teaches English.

# 1

# BUDDHIST PERCEPTIONS OF THE CHRISTIAN USE OF FUNDS IN SRI LANKA

## G. P. V. Somaratna

This article is an analysis of the views held by Buddhists regarding the Christian handling of funds in contemporary Sri Lanka. The author does not attempt to critique the use of funds by Christian pastors, nongovernment organizations (NGOs), or other institutions. Our attention will be limited to the area of Buddhist perceptions in Sri Lanka.

## INTRODUCTION

The historical legacy of Sri Lanka is one of competitive tension between Buddhism and Christianity. Buddhists were dismayed over their predicament in the face of Christians' use of modern facilities for the propagation of the faith ever since the introduction of free religious exercise in Sri Lanka at the beginning of the nineteenth century (De Silva 1974, 69). The British laissez-faire policy of economics and the divide-and-rule policy of administration placed the Buddhists at a disadvantage in this competitive environment. Christians used modern European methods relating to teaching in schools, preaching in public places, printing of polemical material, and the setting up of philanthropic institutions such as hospitals and homes for the aged, the destitute, and juvenile delinquents, to win converts from Buddhism to their brands of Christianity (Malalgoda 1976, 30; Obeyesekere and Gombrich 1990, 202). Christianity, in general, held a preeminent position in the colonial power structure and society. Buddhists have expressed, over and over again, that they want this "historical injustice" corrected. At the same time Buddhist leadership, since the second half of the nineteenth century, has made every possible attempt to counter this debilitating predicament by imitating the Christian institutions in the propagation of their own religion.

Since independence in 1948, popularly elected governments have tried to placate the "grievances" of the Buddhists (Wriggins 1960, 110). Restriction of missionary visas to the country, withdrawal of government assistance to Christian establishments, and the establishment of the government department of Buddha Sasana (Buddhist Studies) have increased Buddhist confidence to control and counter the gains made by Christianity in the past. In addition, the government takeover of denominational schools in 1961 made Christians a beleaguered minority (De Silva 1976, 380). The constitutions of 1972 and 1978 both gave preeminence to Buddhism. Although there was a guarantee of the rights of other religions, state resources were used for uplifting the Buddhist establishment.

In spite of all this, Buddhists have been alarmed by the recent emergence of evangelical and charismatic Christianity, which has made rapid inroads in the Buddhist heartland. Since the 1980s, there have been protests against evangelical groups and their activities in various parts of the country. Newly emerging Christian evangelical groups in Sri Lanka were perceived as a threat to Buddhist dominance of the nation. This was because the institutional framework of these evangelical bodies consisted of churches, parachurch organizations, and several other agencies concentrating on rural development, health, education, and other philanthropic activities.

The Sinhala Buddhist majority has been the most vocal group in complaining against evangelical expansion. However, it should be noted that Sinhala Buddhists see hardly any difference between Catholic and Protestant Christianity. In fact, they include Jehovah's Witnesses, Mormons, Christian Scientists, and Moonies within the category of Christianity. The opinions expressed by Buddhist critics with regard to evangelical activity, as presented in the local mass media and our interviews, show that they do not distinguish the differences among the various groups. All of them are treated interchangeably as Christian. Denominational and doctrinal differences between these groups do not make sense to Buddhists.

In spite of their political power and numerical strength, Buddhists have not been able to match the practice of Christian giving. Christian fundraising methods in Sri Lanka and abroad have surpassed any Buddhist philanthropy. The lack of training in giving for a common cause runs throughout the history of Sri Lanka's Buddhism. Therefore, Buddhists have sought governmental assistance even to manage their own religious establishments (De Silva 1974, 832, 861).

Buddhists complain that they do not have any international network to collect much-needed funds to counter the activities of the Christians, particularly that of the evangelicals (Perera 2004, 22). Buddhists say they have been at a disadvantage when it comes to raising funds for their projects. Buddhist countries like Myanmar, Cambodia, and Laos are poor and unable to fund foreign projects. Others like Japan, Korea, and Thailand have been offered help through their government rather than through NGOs.

Recently, several organizations with Christian affiliations have poured funds into the country to help in natural disasters, development programs, poverty alleviation programs, and evangelization. Therefore, the perception of Buddhists regarding the use of funds by the Christians in Sri Lanka cannot be evaluated merely from a historical point of view, as there are contemporary issues at play.

## BUDDHIST IDEOLOGY

In South Asia, religions act as collective identities. In Sri Lanka, Buddhism has provided not only individual salvation but also secular ideologies. It offers the people of the community a sense of fraternity and an agenda of belonging. Buddhist political groups in Sri Lanka have molded their visions and programs almost exclusively in terms of a Buddhist religious ideology. Therefore the religious issues play a very important political and ideological role in secular political power struggles. This is augmented by the fact that ethnic communities in Sri Lanka are generally identical in religious terms. True Sinhalese are regarded as Buddhists.

It is also noticeable that the Buddhist Sangha has adopted a nationalist stand which condones the policies of violent confrontation in relation to non-Sinhala-Buddhist groups who are perceived as threats to the dominance of Buddhism in the country (Pieris 2001, 10). The view that Sinhalese are Buddhists has created a hostile attitude to Christianity in general, and conversion to Christianity in particular.

## CONVERSION

Religious conversion is the adoption of a new religion that differs from the convert's previous religion. Changing from one denomination to another within the same religion also could be a part of this process (Rambo 1993, 2). Christians consider that conversion requires internalization of the new belief system. It implies a new reference point for the convert's self-identity, and is a matter of belief and social structure which includes both faith and affiliation. Sociologists have noted that "opposition emerges in the ways in which people on the two sides articulate issues of conversion" (Buckser and Glazier 2003, 76). Buddhist critics have indicated that the sinister hand of foreign funds is behind these conversions to Christianity. Buddhists complain that some of their coreligionists are being coerced and converted by Christians (Perera 2004, 20).

## THE BUDDHIST CONCEPT OF GIVING FOR PUBLIC GOOD

Humanitarianism or charity is to give generously without expectation of anything in return. Christian organizations have had the reputation of helping people without any consideration of religious and other social differences. To understand the Buddhist perception of the Christian use of funds, one has to know the Buddhist attitude to charity. *Dāna* is a Pali term meaning "generosity" or "giving." In Buddhism it also refers to the practice of cultivating generosity. It is believed that, by giving, one destroys those acquisitive impulses that ultimately lead to further suffering. In the Pali canon's *Dighajanu Sutta* (Thera 1999, 8.54), generosity (*cāga* for *dāna*) is identified as one of the four traits conditioning happiness and wealth in the next life. These four are faith (*saddhā*), virtue (*sīla*), wisdom (*paññā*), and generosity (*cāga*).

The act of giving will give the donor happiness in the future, in accordance with the karmic law of cause and effect taught by the Buddha (Bodhi 2003, 1). Under these circumstances, the desire to gain merit or reputation, or to win popularity would act as an impulse in the practice of modern Buddhist philanthropy.

In Buddhism, almsgiving is the respect given by a lay Buddhist to a Buddhist monk, nun, spiritually developed person, or other sentient being. It also includes giving to Buddhist institutions such as temples and monasteries. The *suttas* record various motives for exercising generosity. The *Anguttara Nikaya* (Thera 1999, 4.236) enumerates several acts of giving. They are all done for the purpose of gaining merit for benefit in this life or in a future life (*Dhammapada* 24.354).

The Buddhist teaching of the law of karma says:

> For every event that occurs, there will follow another event whose existence was caused by the first, and this second event will be pleasant or unpleasant according to its cause; giving yields benefits in the present life and in lives to come. The most excellent motive for giving is the intention to one's efforts to attain nirvana. (Bodhi 2003, 1)

The purity of the recipient is another factor in the karmic fruitfulness of a gift. The Buddha taught that the worthiest recipients of gifts were the noble ones such as the Buddha himself or those of his disciples, meaning the Sangha (ibid., 5). Therefore giving, in Buddhism, will be interpreted according to cause and effect in this world or in a future life. The karmic theory shows that one is born poor because of one's karmic past. It cannot be altered by outside help, but by one's own accumulation of good karma.

## FLOW OF FUNDS TO CHRISTIAN INSTITUTIONS

Poverty, on the other hand, according to Christianity, is an outrage against humanity. It robs people of dignity, freedom, hope, and power over their own lives. The Christian use of funds in charity is based on that proposition.

There is no reliable statistical information to indicate the exact amount of funds received by Christian institutions in Sri Lanka. Although some funds are received by recognized Christian organizations like Social and Economic Development Centre (SEDEC), National Christian Evangelical Alliance, Sri Lanka (NCEASL), National Christian Council (NCC), and Lanka Evangelical Alliance Development Society (LEADS), there are a large number of churches and individuals receiving money from foreign funds for philanthropic purposes. In the aftermath of the tsunami, a considerable amount of funds came to individuals and individual churches, which were expected to use them for the purpose of helping affected people. It is also well known that funds donated by Christian NGOs, churches, and individuals surpassed all other assistance given to Sri Lanka during the tsunami period. Although the Buddhists were the majority of the population of the country, they did not donate anything close to a small percentage of that amount. In fact, most of the aid distributed by many Buddhist temples in the southern littoral was provided to them by Christian institutions. The ability of Buddhists to use their own funds and exert influence was, therefore, curtailed.

## THE CHRISTIAN VIEW OF CHARITY

Care for the poor and hungry has been part of the Christian "liturgy" from the very beginning. Jesus' statement, "I was hungry and you fed me, thirsty and you gave me a drink; I was a stranger and you received me in your homes, naked and you clothed me; I was sick and you took care of me, in prison and you visited me" (Matt 25:35,36 GNT), has encouraged Christians to help others in need. According to Justin Martyr ([155], 1.67), Sunday services in second-century

Rome included a collection for the poor, and the funds were used to care for orphans, widows, the sick, prisoners, strangers, and "all in need." Assistance was not limited to fellow believers. Even before Christianity became legal in the early fourth century, Christians were recognized for their openhanded generosity which crossed religious boundaries. In this connection, one is reminded of the statement of Julian the Apostate: "These impious Galileans not only feed their own poor, but ours also" (Stern 1980, 549–50). Therefore, Christian charity has tried to relieve poverty and hunger. Care for orphans, widows, and poor families by providing food, clothing, and much love, as well as visiting hospitals and providing medical supplies, and visiting homes for the aged and caring for the old and sick are all part of Christian charity. Humanitarianism or charity in the Christian worldview which encourages generous giving without expectation of anything in return is alien to the karmic views of Buddhist thinking. This is where Buddhists misunderstand Christian charity.

## FUNDS

Many of the funds for Christian charity in Sri Lanka have come from Western Europe, the US, and South Korea. The amount of funds raised locally is insignificant. Many Sri Lankan charities are organizations linked to Christian religious bodies. Numerous NGOs in Sri Lanka, such as World Vision, Samaritan's Purse, Compassion International, Christian Aid, and local organizations like NCEASL, LEADS, ZEDEC, CARITAS, and the NCC, are religious in orientation. The belief among Buddhists is that these nongovernmental organizations with Christian labels receive funds from overseas governments and work in collaboration with governmental agencies at home and abroad (Perera 1999, 106). The NGOs in the past were local counterparts of organizations affiliated with Christian missionary efforts in the British overseas empire (Samaraweera 1997, 4). These NGOs are involved in social service, welfare, and poverty alleviation activities (ibid., 5; Perera 1999, 109). Among their actions, the Buddhist leaders have identified evangelism as a prominent aim (Perera 1999, 115).

## INABILITY TO GRASP FACTS

A Buddhist monk in Kandy stated that "these Catholics have money to build churches and vehicles to travel into villages. We have nothing" (ibid.). In the past, Buddhists have used the methodology of the Christian evangelical institutions to enhance their capability to meet the challenge of the Christian evangelists (Malalgoda 1976, 249; Obeyesekere and Gombrich 1990, 288; De Silva 1974, 344–45). But they are helpless in the wake of recent evangelical expansion in the country. A leading Sri Lankan sociologist, Sasanka Perera, states, "Despite what critics may say, large sources of funds, and aggressiveness alone cannot explain the success of the new evangelists in Sri Lanka" (Perera 1998, 62). The success of Christian evangelism in the recent past is estimated at the popular level on the basis of their relentless activity. He further states that "the kind of reductionist explanations outlined ... are sociologically inadequate to explain the general success of evangelical groups in Sri Lanka" (ibid., 63).

Buddhist institutional organizations lack collective policies or programs to assist refugees, provide shelter for children, or provide rehabilitation services (ibid.). Christian institutions have helped financially where Buddhist temples have been inactive. This has contributed even more to gain converts. In their inability to grasp the reasons for the success of evangelicals, Buddhists have chosen to accuse Christians of what they call "unethical" activities in the country.

## CONVERSION TO CHRISTIANITY

One of the chief accusations of some Buddhist leaders is that Christians are using foreign funds to convert Sinhala Buddhist people. "Many Buddhists seem to believe that new converts are won over by offering them financial and other economic incentives" (Perera 2004, 21). They have indicated that there is a conspiracy against Buddhism by foreign powers with the help of NGOs (LankaWeb, September 22, 2004). This is because most of these funds come from the US and Europe. According to this view, evangelists wage a war to dismantle and destroy Buddhism (LankaWeb, September 23, 2004). They have specially accused "the Christian NGOs operating in Sri Lanka for using devious means to convert innocent Buddhists in villages into Christianity." The use of the word "innocent" meant that these people are poor and lack knowledge. A Buddhist monk in a temple in Colombo stated that the Christian NGOs and those connected with them are funded by foreigners and are fraudulent in their affairs (All Ceylon Buddhist Congress [ACBC] 2009, 106).

Many Buddhists who convert to Christianity often come from socially and economically unfavorable backgrounds. The acceptance of Christianity by some members of the depressed caste known as Rodi had to be economically propped up as the higher castes of the surrounding villagers boycotted their products due to the pressure from Buddhist activists. Some of them have joined the Catholic Church because of the supportive network of the church. Buddhist activists have indicated that Christian evangelicals have even visited the Veddas and tried to convert them after giving them gifts (ibid., 107). These are groups which are not visited by Buddhist monks under normal circumstances because of the karmic explanation of their lowly status.

## MISINTERPRETATION OF GENUINE HELP

Material help given in times of disaster has also been interpreted as bait to convert Buddhists to Christianity. Christian groups have been active at the village level in helping victims of political violence. They have been with them in times of trouble, helping them to cope with grief. Another monk stated that Christians have built houses for tsunami-affected people in Balapitiya. Buddhists believe that these houses have been built in an attempt to convert people by enticing them with material benefits, and that Christians have even offered assistance to monks with a view to spreading Christianity.

Some of the people who receive the benefits of Christian philanthropy and association with evangelicals have turned to Christianity. Buddhist activists interpret this as a gesture of gratitude rather than conviction. They also think that the continued support would eventually attract people to these groups. A Jatika Hela Urumaya (JHU; National Sinhala Heritage) supporter said that converting people would be alright, but the way in which it is being done was wrong, as Christians use money to do so. All the Buddhists interviewed by us expressed the view that there was involvement of foreign funds in the attempt to convert Buddhists to Christianity. Therefore, evangelical expansion in the country has been classified as "unethical conversion." In this way, Buddhist activists have brought this issue to the realm of public debate and have created a Buddhist public hostility to Christianity in general.

## DESTRUCTION OF SINHALESE BUDDHIST CULTURE

Some even indicated that there was a direct effort by Western countries to destroy Buddhism in Sri Lanka. Christian evangelism was presented as a conspiracy against Buddhism. The monks spoke of alleged conspiracies and the cunning tactics used by Christians to convert people. They also stated that "Christianity is losing its foothold in Europe; therefore, they are trying to establish it in Asia using dubious tactics" (LankaWeb, September 22, 2004).

What can be seen here is that Sri Lankan Christians are being directly implicated in this so-called international Christian conspiracy to destroy Buddhism in Sri Lanka. Even more worrying is the fact that certain Buddhists are taking the law into their own hands and attacking both Christian institutions and Christians themselves (ACBC 2009, 110). Some Buddhist monks justified the violence against Christians as necessary in the struggle to save Buddhism from international conspirators (ibid., 111).

## WELFARE IS THE DUTY OF THE STATE

According to the traditional Buddhist view, "the king should take care to satisfy the needy with generosity" (Digha Nikaya 3.66). The Buddhist texts speak of a tenfold code for guidance of kings known as *dasa-raja-dharma*. *Dana* (generosity) and *pariccaga* (selfless service) are two of them (Fausböll 1896, 274). In the tsunami period, when the Salvation Army planned to build one thousand houses in the Hikkaduwa area in the southern part of Sri Lanka, the chief incumbent of the Buddhist temple in the neighborhood objected to it by stating that such work should be undertaken by the state and therefore Christian help was not needed. The reason for the objection is that the people would eventually be attracted to Christianity. The government, on the other hand, had too many irons in the fire and could not attend to individual villages.

## THE NEGATIVE USE OF FUNDS

NGOs are voluntary bodies set up by groups of citizens for a specific purpose. Most of the time their attention is on social service or social and policy intervention (Uyangoda 1995, 104). At the fundamental level of perception, these NGOs have been set up in response to certain needs in the sociopolitical and cultural realms of Sri Lanka. "They have been perceived by those who have been instrumental in setting them up and those who benefit from them as mechanisms of intervention" (Perera 1999, 105). These organizations in general are service oriented. They attempt to address specific issues faced by the people in the country.

One non-Christian writer observed: "In Sri Lanka, Christians are being viewed as vultures nurtured on foreign funds and driven to hunt for the poor mortal souls of the gullible and poverty-stricken non-Christian" (ACBC 2009, 141). Buddhist fears are expressed by a Buddhist writer who states:

Many Sri Lankans are well aware of the poverty-stricken inhabitants of Sinhalese Buddhist villages. They are impressed with the tremendous humanitarian efforts made by the Christian community to improve the conditions in rural areas. They are also aware of the situation in South Korea where an eighty percent Buddhist population was reduced to less than forty percent in just two decades due to Christian evangelism and conversions. (Perera 2004, 21)

Another Buddhist critic has indicated that "missionary activity carried to its logical conclusion will result in Sri Lanka becoming a Christian country. The dagabas, temples, and bo trees will end up like the pyramids of Egypt, only of interest to tourists and historians" (LankaWeb, July 23, 2004).

The rhetoric of betrayal and the need to protect the land is ever present in the Sinhala nationalist discourse, where Sinhalese and Buddhist identities are subsumed to one collapsible identity. The threat is identified as coming from the West, Christianity, and capitalism. The foreign agents are identified as belonging to the NGO sector. Little discrimination is made when speaking of NGOs (Wickramasinghe 1997, 41). A Mahanayake of the Asgiriya Chapter warned that "some non-governmental organizations in this country who receive large amounts of foreign assistance are allegedly engaged in disrobing learned Buddhist monks and providing them secular employment" (Divayina, July 15, 1993).

Such remarks indicate a phobia vis-à-vis foreign aid and Western cultural imperialism, which has spread far beyond the circles of political monks and activists (Sunday Leader, January 14, 1996). There is a view that these groups work in secrecy. Buddhist activists have made use of it to create a phobia among the masses.

The arrival of many aid groups with religious affiliations and the donation of funds by religious organizations from the West provided further ammunition to the argument that such funds were being used for "unethical conversions," particularly of Buddhists and Hindus. Foreign funding for their activities has been viewed as detrimental to indigenous values and the interests of the majority community. The view is that they act as agents of Western countries and entities that have their own political and ideological agendas (Edrisinha 2010, 37). The Buddhist political party, JHU, stated that conversion should not happen outside of proper procedure. This means that the practice of conversion through inducement of material gains made available to the economically deprived is condemned.

The construction of new places of worship and associated buildings give the impression that these groups are swimming in money and expanding at a phenomenal rate. Therefore most of the Buddhist militia has targeted the building activities of Christians irrespective of denominational status.

## ANTINATIONAL

One of the main criticisms levelled against the NGOs is that they engage in antinational activities. Thus, it is alleged, that under the pretext of helping some sections of the population they are putting the entire nation in danger. They have been accused of using their funds to collect information for foreigners (Uyangoda 1995, 650). Christians, both in Sri Lanka and abroad, have been conspicuous for making statements on sociopolitical issues in the country. Although the high-flown statements of church leaders may not have been accompanied by action, Buddhist leaders have construed these statements as antinational. Buddhist critics have stated that the top leadership of the Liberation Tigers of Tamil Eelam (LTTE) was strongly influenced by Christian ideologues. It has come to light that the LTTE has been funded by Tamils living abroad. What is not widely known is that most of the major indirect funding in the LTTE-dominated areas came from US-backed NGOs like World Vision (ACBC 2009, 141). Some NGOs have been branded as fronts for the LTTE. Therefore, on one occasion, a meeting of NGOs was disrupted by a group of Buddhist nationalists (*The Island*, November 17, 1995). Local newspapers like *Divayina* (Sinhala) and *The Island* (English) used this to create an atmosphere of opposition towards Christian NGOs. They have stated that pro-LTTE labels were found on many occasions in these aid packages. In 2006 a villager told a retired Air Force officer that he had been told by a World Vision officer that the display of the World Vision flag would prevent any LTTE attack on their vehicle (ACBC 2009, 150). The implication was that they received assistance from World Vision.

According to the commission report on Christian NGOs, a carefully devised plan has been established to dismantle Buddhism over a long period of time (ibid., 140). Ellawala Medhananda Thera, who was a member of Parliament, addressing the masses at the funeral of Gangodawila Soma Thera, said that if the government does not take steps to stop the devious use of funds by the Christian fundamentalists in the country, the result will be dangerous religious conflict (*Daily News*, December 26, 2003).

Some Buddhist leaders have stated that the growth of Christianity threatens not only the primacy but the very existence of Buddhism (*Sunday Observer*, October 3 and 10, 2004). Therefore they would like the parliament to explicitly prohibit organizations that are not Buddhist from offering aid, regardless of whether there is any evidence that those organizations engage in unethical practices.

## UNETHICAL CONVERSION

"Unethical" or "illegal" conversions are those defined as conversions where something of value has been given in exchange for converting to a different faith. It has long been indicated that money has been used for conversions. This is particularly noted as "to buy land, fertilizer, seed, and food, or free education for children" (Perera 2004, 24). A Sri Lankan newspaper reported:

> We are aware that certain Christian sects receive massive sums of money from America and other foreign countries to be spent lavishly in remote villages comprised of only poor Buddhists in a bid to convert them to their faith by exploiting their meager economic conditions, assisting in their marriages, and helping them to secure employment. (*The Island*, May 20, 1993)

A long list of alleged material inducement offered to various people in numerous parts of Sri Lanka is reported in the commission report inquiring into unethical financial transfers in Sri Lanka published in 2009. This report says that the practice of enticing the hungry and sick to Christianity with offers of food and medicine may not be illegal, but is hardly ethical, especially given that so many of the poor people have little or no understanding of the concept of religious "conversion." World Vision and evangelistic organizations funded by the USA are at the top of the list. Their approach to and methods of assistance are founded on the "give and take" business principle, rather than on an altruistic humanitarian philosophy. Their generous "benevolence" is laden with strings. In terms of real value, what they give is negligible when compared to what they seek and get. What they do at the grassroots level among the crisis-ridden, poverty-stricken, distressed, and desperate people do not qualify as humanitarian or charitable efforts (ACBC 2009, 4).

## THE BUDDHIST VIEW OF CONVERSION

The purpose of Buddhist preaching is to get listeners to accept what is taught. It does not stress conversion. All the discourses of the Buddha end with the statement that the listeners rejoiced over what the Buddha said. One cannot come across a term equivalent to conversion in Buddhist literature. However, the new Buddhists traditionally expressed faith in the Three Gems: Buddha, Dharma, Sangha, and became followers of the Buddha. The understanding of conversion in the Buddhist tradition is different from that in Christianity. Buddhists often hold multiple religious identities, combining the religion with worship of Hindu deities and animistic practices.

According to the report of the Buddhist commission of 2009, the average Sri Lankan villager is uneducated, and they would convert for the slightest material benefit that they could obtain (ibid., 112). Even if they converted for material benefits and do not really follow the religion, their children would follow the religion in the future. Thus, with time, the numbers of Buddhists would drop so that they would constitute a small percentage.

The same report states that an education program showing villagers the true intentions of evangelism is gradually beginning to surface in rural areas. World Vision's "Mustard Seed Project" in the Ratnapura District was halted when their surreptitious intentions were brought to light. Their comment was: "We cannot feed individuals and then let them go to hell." There are currently several lawsuits in Sri Lanka for "illegal conversion" (ibid., 114).

## A NATIONAL PROBLEM

The information derived from these interviews makes it clear that Buddhists consider this a national problem. The way Christians use their funds is perceived by Buddhists as a threat to the nation of Sri Lanka. They consider it as a foreign conspiracy to destroy Buddhism in Sri Lanka. Christian nations in the Western world are seen as the largest culprits. The foreigners involved in churches are viewed as invaders. Buddhists who convert are traitors. The perception is that these activities are done by foreigners. Often they are referred to as coming from the US, even though there are some missionaries who come from India and Korea as well (ibid., 507).

## CRITICISM

Buddhist criticism is that NGOs have become miniature personal kingdoms for egotistical and power hungry individuals. Some NGOs strictly run as small pockets of colonies with rigid master-slave relationships between the "NGO leader" and "NGO workers and beneficiaries." The top managers act like dictators with blatant disregard for the rules of state law, local wisdom, cultural values, fiscal responsibility, and administrative integrity. They have taken it upon themselves to believe that they are above and beyond any rules and regulations set up by civil society, the government, or the NGO community to guide their conduct. Irrational behavior, contempt towards the laws of the land, and arrogance are rampantly displayed. Buddhist monks have indicated that NGOs are able to get away with their activities by using racism and religion as shields to protect themselves. The country's wretched lot—children, disaster victims, beggars, the old, the sick, and other underprivileged souls—have become their pawns in their desire for callous dominance.

## THE TSUNAMI

Buddhist critics have indicated that the tsunami disaster provides good examples of the predatory behavior of Christian organizations towards helpless and vulnerable people. The intentional targeting of the most vulnerable children has annoyed some. One Sri Lankan writer has stated:

> What these people need is assistance to recover from their tragic state brought about by the loss of their loved ones, their dwellings, their material possessions, and income. They have not lost their Buddhism or Hinduism or Islam to be assisted with another religion, particularly with a religion that is being discarded in most of the Western world. (Commission Report on Unethical Conversions 2009, 109)

## THE CHURCH'S DENIAL OF UNETHICAL CONVERSION

The Ampitiya Conference of the Catholic hierarchy stated that the conversion of Buddhists was not the agenda of the church in Sri Lanka. The present Archbishop of Colombo, Cardinal Malcolm Ranjit, categorically denied any involvement of funds in evangelism. He stated, "I wish to state clearly that the Catholic Church is not engaged in such tactics" (*Catholic Messenger*, August 1, 1993). Similar statements have been made by the National Christian Council, whose members are from traditional Christian churches.

Another allegation of the Buddhists is the attempts at "offering material inducements to make Christians, which they refer to as 'buying' converts." This usage is similar to the term "rice Christian," the pejorative term used in the past to refer to someone who has formally declared himself a Christian for material benefits. The term comes from Asian countries such as India, in which local populations suffering economically under Western colonialism and unequal treaties nominally converted to Christianity in hopes of getting food from Christian missionaries. This has been categorically rejected by all Christian groups. Evangelicals vehemently deny the validity of this statement. Their view is that no "genuine Christian" would emerge as a result of monetary aid. They argue that many of these new Christians actually lose material benefits which they used to enjoy before they accepted Christianity, on account of leaving Buddhism. Nevertheless, Buddhists insist that inducement is being used (Dhammika 2004). Concerns have been expressed both by Christian missionaries and by those opposed to Christian missions that people in these situations are nominally converting to Christianity in order to receive charity or material advancements.

## UNDISCIPLINED GROUP OF PEOPLE LAVISHLY USING FUNDS

According to some critics:

> Evangelical churches have enthusiastically adopted the outlook of big corporations making high pressure sales techniques, blanket advertising, door to door canvassing, etc. As a result of this, people who would have never changed their religion are now doing so. The process of religious switching has been transformed from being a personal and individual one to being one artificially induced by external forces. (ibid.)

The annual report of the Young Men's Buddhist Association (YMBA), 1989–1990, stated that a subtle proselytizing campaign was being carried out through insidious methods. It involved giving money and other inducements to inveigle innocent and poverty-stricken Buddhists into changing their religion. Funds were coming in from foreign lands to promote this anti-Buddhist activity (YMBA 1989–1990, 49). This could add to the unethical conversion of the poor to Christianity by evangelical Christian sects which were doing so freely (*Sunday Times*, May 10, 1998, 11).

## AN OCCUPATION PAID FOR BY AMERICANS

A Sri Lankan sociologist has stated that modern evangelistic groups have made this island a base of operation in the competitive vocation of soul saving. "Most evangelical churches come from the USA, and in some ways they are more influenced by distinctly American values than they are by those of that gentleman of Nazareth" (Perera 2004, 24). Some cynics have stated that the pastors who serve in Buddhist villages are paid by imperialists. They take photographs of their congregations and send them abroad to seek funds (ACBC 2009, 589–607 passim). According to some speculators, when they convert more people, they are paid more from those foreign funds. They are provided with money to develop infrastructure such as church buildings, libraries, preschools, and to provide help to aid institutions, and so on.

## CONVERSION CAUSED BY MATERIAL BENEFITS

In the Buddhist perception among the modern Christian churches in Sri Lanka, the Assemblies of God stands out as an institution using funds to convert Buddhists. Its membership now stands above that of the Church of Ceylon, which so far has been the largest Protestant denomination. Their churches are found in all parts of the country. The majority of their believers and the pastors are from a Buddhist background. Their parents and other relatives may still be Buddhists. They have built churches in predominantly Buddhist villages and towns. In 1992 the Sri Lankan government conducted an inquiry entitled the "NGO Commission." As a result of this inquiry, the Assemblies of God denomination was blamed for the fraudulent use of funds obtained from foreign sources to entice Buddhists to the Christian faith.

The other group that received castigation from the NGO Commission for using funds to convert people was World Vision Lanka. As a result, World Vision has reduced their evangelical work to a minimum. They have even employed non-Christians in their workforce with a view to countering the arguments of the Buddhist lobby.

## UNETHICAL BEHAVIOR

Although the mainline Christian institutions are careful in managing their funds, overenthusiastic evangelists have been found to be using funds inappropriately, leaving room for Buddhist criticism. There are many mushroom Christian sects and fanatical groups that are not concerned about the greater glorification of the Christian faith. They seem to act as business operations or impervious cults whose tactics are aimed towards augmenting their numbers. According to a newspaper report: "They have used proselytism and somewhat impure methods devised to attract poor unsuspecting individuals by virtue of their impoverished circumstances" (*The Island*, February 2, 2000).

## PASTORS' LIFESTYLE

The money is supposed to go to charitable work, but some have claimed that a fair portion of it is funneled away into the pockets of the pastors. The lifestyle of certain pastors is disproportionately higher than that of their believers, indicating the use of foreign funds (ACBC 2009, 473). In some churches where the prosperity gospel is preached, the accusation is that the pastors exhort worshipers to give generously if they want the Lord's blessing.

## POSITIVE VIEWS

Although the views expressed by Buddhist scholars, observers, and monks give a negative light regarding the Christian use of funds in philanthropic activities, the people at the grassroots level have a different opinion. Their views are not what the Buddhist lobby wants to hear. The opinion makers, on the other hand, are elites who see Christian philanthropy in a negative light. The poor and marginalized, who have received such assistance, have expressed their gratefulness in our interviews. However, their views are not highlighted in the mass media—probably because of the Buddhist national bias.

For example, when on September 11, 2006, an agent from the Mica Network in the Netherlands paid a visit to a tsunami village built by the NCEASL in Galle, the people almost worshiped him. This village was built by the NCEASL with the help of their funds. The people in the village are mostly Buddhists. There are houses given to Muslim, Tamil, and Hindu families as well. The recipients were selected by the District Secretariat of Galle (NCEASL 2010). All these houses were built in Buddhist areas. The Tittagala housing scheme was built by the NCEASL with the help of the Dutch Reformed Church of Sri Lanka and the Samaritan's Purse organization (which is represented as an aggressive proselytizing agency). In addition to the houses, the occupants were given training for self-employment. The villagers are extremely grateful to the NCEASL and have expressed their willingness to defend them in the event of an attack by the Buddhist militia.

During the time of the tsunami, the NCEASL gave support to all those affected in the Galle area. Similar action was taken in other areas as well. At the outset of the disaster, all the organizations allowed temporary residence to the people. However, even the Buddhists are not reluctant to state that the continued support and the lasting help were given by Christian organizations.

There are many reports where Christians have been praised by the victims of the tsunami-affected areas. The evangelical groups were in the forefront of relief work. The traditional churches and parachurch organizations also did their best according to their capacity. However, the evangelicals were able to deliver goods faster than others because many evangelical churches were under a senior pastor who could make decisions and attend to problems immediately. Other organizations were not as quick because of their internal formalities and audit requirements.

## CONCLUSION

The Buddhist perception of the Christian use of funds shows a clash of two different religious views. One is based on the mechanical karmic view of life, while the other is based on a relational, God-centered view of life. Christian institutions of help have been founded on the Golden Rule: "Do unto others as you would have others do unto you." It is true that the Christians use their funds for philanthropic activities which may have evangelical implications. However, the allegation that Christians use these funds with a divisive motive to dismantle the Buddhist civilization is far-fetched. Buddhists worry that the operations of evangelical groups will eventually bring their religion to a minority status in the country, following the example of South Korea. The basic point in the agenda of Buddhist activists is that this phase of new evangelical drive will reduce the percentage of Buddhists in the country. To this, they have been able to add the real and imaginary use of funds by Christians in their philanthropic activities.

# REFERENCES

All Ceylon Buddhist Congress. 2009. *The report of the commission inquiring to the unethical and devious ways of converting the Buddhists to other religions.* Colombo: All Ceylon Buddhist Congress.

Ammerman, Nancy T. 1994. The dynamics of Christian fundamentalism: An introduction. In *Accounting for fundamentalisms: The dynamic character of movements,* eds. Martin E. Marty and R. Scott Appleby, 13–17. Vol. 4 of The Fundamentalism Project. Chicago: University of Chicago Press.

Bhikkhu, Thanissaro, trans. 1995. Dighajanu (Vyagghapajja) Sutta: To Dighajanu (AN 8.54). Access to Insight. http://www.accesstoinsight.org/tipitaka/an/an08/an08.054.than.html.

Bodhi, Bhikkhu. 2003. *Dana: The practice of giving.* Kandy, Sri Lanka: Wheel Publications.

Brouser, Steve, Paul Gifford, and Susan D. Rose. 1996. South Korea: Modernization with a vengeance; Evangelization with the modern edge. In *Exporting the American gospel: Global Christian fundamentalism,* eds. Steve Brouser, Paul Gifford, and Susan D. Rose, 105–130. New York: Routledge.

Buckser, Andrew, and Stephen D. Glazier. 2003. *The anthropology of religious conversion.* Lanham, MD: Rowman & Littlefield.

Caplan, Lionel. 1995. Certain knowledge: The encounter of global fundamentalism and local Christianity in urban South India. In *The pursuit of certainty: Religious and cultural formulation,* ed. Wendy James, 92–111. London: Routledge.

*Catholic Messenger.* August 1, 1993. Colombo: Gnanartha Pradeepaya.

Colby, Gerard, and Charlotte Dennett. 1995. *Thy will be done: The conquest of the Amazon; Nelson Rockefeller and evangelism in the age of oil.* New York: HarperCollins.

Commission report on unethical conversions. 2009. Paper presented to the Most Venerable Maha Sangha and Buddhist Public, Colombo, Sri Lanka. January 6.

*Daily News.* December 26, 2003. Colombo: Lakehouse Newspapers.

David, Morgan. 1997. The pressure to go mega. *Direction,* November. Colombo: Ceylon Every Home Crusade.

De Silva, K. M. 1974. *University of Ceylon, history of Ceylon.* Vol. 3. Colombo: University of Ceylon Press.

———, ed. 1976. *Sri Lanka: A survey.* London: Oxford University Press.

*Dhammapada.* www.tipitaka.net/tipitaka/dhp/verseload.php?verse=204.

Dhammika, Ven. 2004. Conversion: Unethical and otherwise; Buddhist view. *The Island,* July 15.

Dhirasekera, Jothiya, ed. 1989. *Encyclopaedia of Buddhism.* Vol. 4. Colombo: Government of Sri Lanka.

*Divayina.* July 15, 1993. Colombo: Upali Newspapers.

Edrisinha, Rohan. 2010. Sri Lanka. *International Journal of Not-for-Profit Law* 12, no. 3 (May): 35–40.

Fausböll, M. V., ed. 1896. *Jataka with commentary.* Vol. 3. London: Pali Text Society.

Goonatilake, Susantha. 2006. *Recolonisation: Foreign funded NGOs in Sri Lanka.* Delhi: Sage Publications.

*The Island.* May 20, 1993. Colombo: Upali Newspapers.

———. November 17, 1995. Colombo: Upali Newspapers.

———. February 2, 2000. Colombo: Upali Newspapers.

Janakaratne, K. K. I. 1994. *Attraction of Catholics to Christian fundamentalist sects: A sociological study on sect formation.* BA diss., University of Colombo.

Jones, Ken. 1981. *Buddhism and social action.* Kandy, Sri Lanka: Wheel Publication Society.

Kiblinger, Kristin Beise. 2005. *Buddhist inclusivism: Attitudes towards religious others.* Burlington, VT: Ashgate.

LankaWeb. http://www.lankaweb.com/.

Malalgoda, Kitisiri. 1976. *Buddhism in Sinhalese society 1750–1900: A study of religious revival and change.* Berkeley: University of California Press.

Martyr, Justin. [155?] *The first apology of Justin: Addressed to the Emperor Antoninus Pius.* Trans. Roberts-Donaldson. Repr., Early Christian Writings, 2001. http://www.earlychristianwritings.com/text/justinmartyr-firstapology.html.

National Christian Evangelical Alliance, Sri Lanka. 2010. *NCEASL directory.* Dehiwela, Sri Lanka: National Christian Evangelical Alliance, Sri Lanka.

Obeyesekere, Jananath, and Richard Gombrich. 1990. *Buddhism transformed: Religious change in Sri Lanka.* New York: Princeton University Press.

Perera, Sasanka. 1998. *New evangelical movements and conflict in South Asia: Sri Lanka and Nepal in perspective.* Policy Studies 5. Colombo: Regional Centre for Strategic Studies.

———. 1999. Non government organizations in Sri Lanka: The dynamics, the impact, the rhetoric, and the politics. *Dialogue* 26: 104–24.

———. 2004. *Living with torturers and other essays of intervention: Sri Lankan society, culture, and politics in perspective.* Colombo: International Centre for Ethnic Studies.

Pieris, Aloysius. 2001. The impossibility of intolerance: Buddhist perspective. *Dialogue* 28: 1–17.

Pieris, Kamalika. 2000. Christian conversion in Buddhist Sri Lanka. *The Island,* March 8.

Rambo, Lewis R. 1993. *Understanding religious conversion.* New Haven: Yale University Press.

Samarasekera, Gerald de S. 2004. LTTE and the Christian church. LankaWeb. http://www.lankaweb.com/news/items04/110904-2.html.

Samaraweera, Vijaya. 1997. *Politics, national security, and the vibrancy of NGOs.* Colombo: Law and Society Trust.

Samuel, Vinay. 1998. Christian mission in contemporary Asia. Paper presented at the Christian Conference of Asia/Mission Unity Dialogue, January 17–19, Bangalore.

Shah, Saubhagya. 1993. The gospel come to the Hindu kingdom. *Himal* (September–October).

Shashikamar, V. K., and Mayablushan Neguenkar. 2004. Preparing for the harvest. *Tehelka* (February 7).

Stanley, Harriet. 1994. Culture and meaning: Personal reflection on Christmas in Nepal. *Mirror* (magazine of the United Nations Women's Organization, Nepal).

Stern, M. 1980. *Greek and Latin authors on Jews and Judaism: From Tacitus to Simplicius.* Jerusalem: Israel Academy of Sciences and Humanities.

*Sunday Leader.* January 14, 1996. Ratmalana, Sri Lanka: Sunday Leader Newspapers.

*Sunday Observer.* October 3 and 10, 2004. Colombo: Lakehouse Newspapers.

*Sunday Times.* May 10, 1998. Colombo: Wijeya Newspapers.

Thera, Nyanaponika. 1999. *Anguttara nikaya.* Lanham, MD: Altamira.

Thero, Kollupitiye Samadhindriya. 2005. Tilling the mission fields in Sri Lanka. February 6. LankaWeb. http://www.lankaweb.com/news/items05/060205-5.html.

Thomas, Paul. 2002. *Human rights and religious conversion.* Delhi: Media House.

Uyangoda, Jayadeva. 1995. *Life under the milkwood: Women workers in rubber plantations.* Colombo: Women's Education and Research Centre.

Wickramasinghe, Nira. 1997. *Humanitarian relief organisations and challenges to sovereignty: The case of Sri Lanka.* Colombo: Colombo Regional Centre for Strategic Studies.

Wriggins, William Howard. 1960. *Ceylon: Dilemmas of a new nation.* Princeton: Princeton University Press.

*YMBA* (Young Men's Buddhist Association) *Journal.* 1989–1990.

Yu, Carver T. 1998. The Bible and culture in the shaping of Asian theology. Paper presented at the Christian Conference of Asia/Mission Unity Dialogue, January 17–19, Bangalore.

# 2

# PERSONAL REFLECTIONS ON FINANCIAL RESPONSIBILITY OF MISSIONARIES AND INDIGENOUS CHURCHES

## Alex G. Smith

Complementing one another, greed and control are the insidious twin vices plaguing humans from times ancient to modern. While affluence and poverty coexist in rich and poor, the combined corruption of greed and power are common to both classes. Despite the ageless, perennial disparities between "haves and have-nots," both the deprived and the wealthy commonly share this thirst for control and commodities. These economic inequities have confronted missionaries on every continent in all ages. From time immemorial, power and greed fed the appetites of pharaohs, emperors, czars, sultans, kings, and popes. Their lifestyles, palaces, castles, homes, monasteries, and treasuries told the tale. The Buddhist Empress Dowager Cixi (1835–1908) of China's Qing Dynasty ate 150-dish dinners "with golden chopsticks" (Newsweek 2009, 6). Meanwhile most of the subjects of such rulers lived in abject squalor.

During a recent six-week period in late 2010, Indian authorities uncovered four massive corruption scandals linked to the current Congress party, involving billions of dollars in lost government revenues (Bendern and Chakravorty 2010, 1–2). *Baksheesh* (money) drives Indian culture, and bribery makes the Asian world turn. Recent charges accused political leaders in Korea, Japan, and China of embarrassing corruption. But the West has become no better than the East. The greedy vitiation exposing immoral corruption in Wall Street, Enron, AIG, big banks, and their CEOs is unconscionable. The human lust after wealth observed in Genghis Khan of Mongolia and Imelda Marcos in the Philippines matches huge rip-offs of American Bernard Madoff, whose Ponzi schemes made off with billions of trusting investors' savings. Insider trading on global stock exchanges threatens world financial markets, nations, and communities.

The Lord's servants were not immune from avarice. Because King Solomon chose to ask for wisdom, God blessed him with uncountable riches also. However, this affluence along with his multiple foreign wives and innumerable horses contributed to his weakening in the end (1 Kgs 10:14–11:43). The Bible records God's judgments on the greedy ambitions of Lot, Abram's nephew (Gen 13:7–13); Gehazi, Elijah's servant (2 Kgs 5:20–27); and Ananias and Sapphira (Acts 5:1–10).

## INTRODUCTION TO THE FOCUS

Our primary concern suggests dependence on outside resources is detrimental to the selfhood, dignity, identity, and personal ownership of the local church, detracting from its true mission and reducing its motivation, initiative, and control over its operations in the community. Missionaries and foreign donors also need to exhibit thoughtful models for the local church, but must be careful in the roles, policies, and behaviors they adopt.

## MISSIONARY DILEMMA: WHEN TO GIVE OR NOT?

Confusion often confounds new missionary arrivals on their new fields of service overseas. Being overwhelmed with culture shock is prevalent and normal. The challenge of different economics, deprived public conditions, and the prevalence of poverty blatantly surround them. Beggars galore, many terribly disfigured by leprosy, tug at their hearts. Learning when to give and when not to give, whom to give to and whom not to, add emotional stress to pitiful situations. Stretched on the horns of a dilemma, missionaries frequently struggle with these economic inequalities.

### Exposure to the Issues

In 1963 on our first exposure to Asia, our ship berthed at Bombay. As my wife and I walked the dirty, dusty streets, we noticed a woman up ahead with a baby in arms. As we got closer we saw her deliberately pinch her tiny baby until it cried out in the most piteous pain. As her mother pushed her alms bowl in our faces, we saw the baby's limbs were terribly disfigured. Later we were told the mother had broken her baby's arms and legs and allowed them to heal in those ugly twisted positions in order to get more pity and money from the foreigners. Sadly, the dark places of many lands are full of the habitations of violence and cruelty (Ps. 74:20).

During our first term, the workers on our missionary team independently gave at will to individuals or families in need. This sometimes produced inequities, confusion, and jealousy in the community. Later, as a team who prayed together a half day every week, we agreed to discuss situations of financial help with the whole team first, before any distribution was made. When to give, to whom to give, and how much to give became a mutual decision of the team.

We worked mainly with rural folk who were often from poor, financially disadvantaged communities with families struggling particularly because of leprosy. A wise senior missionary raised a vital question from his experience, related to a psychological perspective: "Was it right to give some people money that would only reinforce their negative self-image and lower their self-worth? How could we avoid causing dependence rather than independence?" This produced a key principle for the team's input, namely to discuss what effects outside giving would have on the individual and family. What might be detrimental? What would be beneficial? How might giving affect their spiritual life? We prayed, discussed, and worked through these questions before deciding to give. Too often giving without thought does more damage than considering what will produce real assistance. As the old proverb says, "It is better to teach them to fish than to give them a fish daily." How does our giving build people up so they function fully as responsible humans in dignity, created in God's image?

I remember a youthful American Peace Corps worker in Thailand who decided that he needed to alleviate the poor sanitary conditions in the community to which he was assigned in northeast Isaan. He purchased some materials, built strategically placed toilets, and taught the people the reason and the purpose for their use. After a few years he left and returned to USA. A year or two later he decided to come and visit to see how well his project was working. He was shocked to see that no one was using the toilets, except to store equipment in them. He was upset. As an outsider and advocate for the peoples' good, he had tried his best to improve conditions, with little effect it seemed. While he was with the Isaan people, it worked. When he left, they simply reverted to their old ways.

By way of contrast, in our area there lived an elderly, respected village headman. He had attended the Thai provincial governor's workshop on the problem of village sanitation. Because his people were frequently sick from dysentery, he knew his village needed remedial action. He built a toilet for his own family, and they began to use it. As time passed, the villagers noticed that his family was seldom sick from dysentery. They asked him what the secret was. The headman waited for the right opportunity to educate his people. He then told them about the main causes of water pollution, the reason for the toilet, and how to build one. Soon each family had built their own toilet with their own materials and labor. They began using them to the value of the whole community. The difference had been the local leader who was not only a respected insider but also an active innovator and model who knew his community.

## Rethinking Experience

On our first term, my wife and I along with our two small sons frequently traveled on trains to or through a large town in central Thailand. Every time we noticed a particular older man who shuffled along the platform with a walking stick, begging and looking sadly forlorn. We often gave him something. One day out of pity for his hunger, our boys gave him their sandwiches which we had prepared for the journey. We watched as he opened them and threw them on the ground disdainfully. This shocked and hurt our sons and us. Some local folk told us that this beggar was in fact a wealthy townsman, who owned half the city's property. We had noticed that as trains arrived he changed his normal gait into a shuffling, stiff-legged man using a rough walking stick as he pushed his begging bowl towards foreigners and Thai alike. We decided not to give any more to this man, who usually straightened up and walked normally after the train left the station.

We endeavored to live at the same level as the people and used rented premises equivalent to teachers, the ascribed role they gave us. We ate foods from the local markets, wore clothes made and bought in Thai shops, and traveled on public transportation, yet as foreigners we were still seen as wealthy. Though many thought of us as well-off, they did not expect us to live entirely at the exact same level as themselves.

The economic contrast is often magnified when missionaries return to their homelands on home assignments. After living a simplified life of limited choices in Asia, my wife at first became almost immobilized by reverse culture shock when she went into American supermarkets to buy groceries. Sometimes she would leave without buying much at all, confused by the multitude of choices, varieties of goods, and comparatively high prices so different from rural Asia's sufficient, sparse products.

## The Hardest Thing: To Keep Balanced

In later years we lived near a famous Christian school. As we walked by well-dressed students from upper-crust families, they often extended a hand out to us asking for one *baht*—a paltry five cents then. One day one of these students asked for ten *baht*. When I asked him why an increased ten, he replied in Thai, "*Nam mun khyn*" ("Gas prices have increased"); inflation!

Keeping balanced is often complex. It was rumored that Hudson Taylor traveled third class in China because there was no fourth class. Interestingly, Dwight L. Moody, the celebrated evangelist (1837–1899), received considerable criticism for taking the first-class coach on overnight trains from city to city. He replied that the Lord's work to which he was committed and the thousands of souls he would touch for eternity required his best-rested efforts, only made possible by traveling in first-class sleepers. Sometimes following wisdom is better than pinching pennies. In one's own culture, that is easier to do than when an alien overseas.

Since Buddhist monks got special discounts for train travel in Thailand, the Thai Department of Religious Affairs also extended that privilege to missionaries as religious workers. But after a time our agency and others decided not to take advantage of that provision. It portrayed a form of class distinction which differentiated between "priest and people" and discriminated between local believers and their missionary servants. Besides, some Christians also misused this privilege, projecting a poor witness to Buddhist society.

Mission executives occasionally face difficult decisions on expending money. When Muslim bandits kidnapped our friends and fellow workers, Minka Hanskampp and Margaret Morgan, while they were treating leprosy patients in a midday clinic in south Thailand in the mid 1970s, they asked a large ransom for their release. Since paying ransom would likely open the door to making all missionaries face similar treatment and extortion, agency leaders refused to pay, even though it meant the probable murder of God's servants. Three months later the limp, slaughtered bodies of these two nurses were found dumped into a ravine. To keep balanced under moral pressures and critical times is not always easy.

## UNDERSTANDING BIBLICAL INSTRUCTIONS ON FINANCES

The Bible has much to say about poverty, wealth, money, and its uses. Here we can only touch on a few appropriate, related references. There is advantageous value in having plentiful resources. But neither penury nor wealth equate with holiness or determine righteousness. How we utilize them is a privileged stewardship. Being rich per se is not condemned. However, riches tend to distract us from total dependence on God. They often entice us into avarice. Dire consequences and dangers follow when we foolishly misuse funds.

## Principles for Avoidance: Vapors

Covetousness is a key human trap. Christ instructed his followers, "Beware, and be on your guard against every form of greed" (Luke 12:15 NASB). He then told of the misguided rich man who decided to pull down his barns and build larger ones to house his abundant harvests. He put value on his grain and property above his own soul and spirit. Consequently, when God called his soul to himself that night, the rich man lost all. A key point Jesus explained is that life is more than food, clothing, or money, so we are not to be anxious for material gain but rather for spiritual health by seeking first the kingdom of God (Luke 12:15–34).

James penned a similar view, indicating that temporal life is uncertain and compares to "a vapor" that can easily disappear in an instant (Jas 4:13–16). The hymn writer Isaac Watts penned a complementing Pauline perspective (Phil 3:7–10): "When I survey the wondrous cross … my richest gain I count but loss."

To obsess, covet, or crave riches is to be avoided at all costs, because "the love of money is the root of all evil" (1 Tim 6:10 KJV). Those who thirst for gold and its accumulation may well remember that we are born naked and when we die we take not one red cent with us into eternity.

At a northern Thai airport, I once was checking in along with my pastor when I noticed goods wrapped in Thai newspapers sitting right on the airline desk in front of me. Thinking someone may have misplaced it, I picked it up, only to be surprised at its extreme weight. Turning to my pastor as I looked inside the newsprint, I whispered, "Guess what? This is gold." Incredulously he laughed and took a skeptical look. Wrapped in the paper were two large bars of pure gold! Even at $350 an ounce then, it was worth about $300,000. Today, with gold over $1,200 an ounce, its worth would be over $1 million. I asked the service representative if anyone had reported something lost. She replied negatively. I had no moral dilemma and handed it over for safekeeping. Later we realized it may have been drug pay-off money. Even the largest sum of money I have ever had in my hand could not entice me to go against my moral convictions.

## Principles for Adoption: Values

Jesus taught his disciples to follow higher values than normally expected. "It is more blessed to give than to receive" (Acts 20:35). "Give to the one who asks you" (Matt 5:42). "Freely you have received; freely give" (Matt 10:8). The world says, "Get," not "Give." But do these verses encourage indiscriminate giving, or do they remind us that kingdom attitudes must reflect that all we have is the Lord's, not ours? Tithing for Jews was the law's requirement. But for Christians, all we are and have belong to the Lord (Rom 11:35,36; 1 Cor 6:19,20). God and people are more important than things. The poor widow in her abandoned dedication to God gave two mites, all that she had to live on (Luke 21:1–4). Paul commends the churches of Macedonia for giving so liberally out of their deep poverty and of themselves to God (2 Cor 8:1–5).

Christ sent his disciples out across the Israelite countryside, instructing them to take "no money in your belts" (Mark 6:8). Take nothing except a mere staff; no bread, no begging bag, no money! In essence Christ commanded total dependence on God alone. This indicates that missionaries are to depend entirely on God too, not necessarily just on their supporters. Yet they are not to be irresponsible. They ought to prepare provision for overseas service through expectant faith and a sense of responsibility under God's great providence. The apostles did not refuse support or gifts, but reminded all that godliness with contentment was great gain (1 Tim 6:6).

Jesus warned his disciples not to lay up "for yourselves treasures upon earth" … but to lay it up in heaven, "for where your treasure is, there will your heart be also." You "cannot serve God and mammon," namely riches (Matt 6:19–24 KJV). These values are extreme ones, those of God's kingdom. Believers are called to a revolutionary change of attitude and perspective, from the material to the spiritual focus, from gold to God, and from greed on earth to gain in heaven.

## Problems of False Prosperity Gospel

In some circles of modern Christianity, a prosperity gospel is being preached, offering wealth, health, and happiness as the right of believers. One motto is: "Name it and claim it." The Bible, particularly the Old Testament, speaks of God's blessing, protection, and plenty for Jehovah's true people through his providence, grace, and mercy. But the proponents of the prosperity gospel declare these to be the absolute rights of believers. The impression given is that Christians should be materially rich, always healthy, and extremely happy, meaning the gospel is paved with a bed of roses without the thorns. Proponents of the prosperity gospel assume that believers anywhere who are not rich, healthy, and happy are inadequate members. The reality is that the majority of Christians worldwide are economically poor, though redemption and its consequent transformation also bring changes producing economic and spiritual lift.

The Apostle Paul declares that not many wise, mighty, or noble enter Christ's kingdom (1 Cor 1:26–31). In most cases the wise, mighty, and noble are the ones most likely to be economically advantaged (Prov 14:24). Fortunately, the Scripture does not state that no wise, mighty, noble, or rich followed Christ. This modern message of prosperity gives to many a false assurance, erroneous promises, and a faulty base for building a kingdom of righteousness. Holiness, not riches, is the mark of Christ's people. Righteousness, not possessions (nor income levels), distinguishes true followers from false.

Buddhist and other leaders and their governments often accuse and condemn those missionaries who use money to buy converts from other religions. This is largely a false charge, but unfortunately there are some who violate the principle of godly propagation by using pecuniary means to attract followers, a practice which we unequivocally condemn.

## BUDDHISM AND FINANCIAL IMPLICATIONS

In Buddhist Scriptures there is little reference to direct teachings on money. One key exception is noted when Uggaha, grandson of Mendaka, who was "a fabulously rich man with magic powers," asked Buddha to counsel his daughters so they would act appropriately to their husbands and parents to whom they went upon marriage. In relation to "the money, corn, silver and gold that our husbands bring home," Buddha advised them: "We will keep safe watch and ward over it, and act as no robber, thief, carouser, wastrel therein" (Hare 2006, 28–30). Thus Buddha taught careful stewardship, responsibility, and accountability in regards to resources.

### Karma and Greed or Desires for Money

The sutras and Tipitaka are full of stories related to the negative results of peoples' greed, desires, passion, and craving. Thus karma detrimentally operates in their future lives. While money is not specifically singled out for emphasis, its painful control is implied in Buddhist stories such as the greedy and foolish monkey who gets his four limbs and snout stuck in the trap of pitch, only to end up as a meal for the hunter (Woodward 2005, 127). A basic prohibition of the five *sila* of morality prohibits stealing, enjoining, "Don't take what is not given."

Still in contrast to Christianity, formal organized relief agencies are comparatively few among the majority of Buddhist sects. This has begun to change in the last decade, particularly in Taiwan. During natural disasters, seldom are large organized relief efforts by Buddhist monks or the Sangha observed in action. One reason is that Buddhists often think that the cause behind those affected unfortunates is primarily their own inescapable karma. Furthermore, many folk Buddhists fear that helping those in devastating dire straits will provoke the bad spirits, causing death to attack them and their families.

## Buddhist Monks and Money

Buddha certainly accepted gifts of money, partook of lavish feasts prepared by devotees, received daily offerings of food, as well as welcomed presents of monks' robes and other property. He encouraged his followers to give alms to the poor, make offerings to the Sangha, and do many meritorious deeds, most of which requires the dispensing of money. He also endorsed the transfer of merit to ancestors and to others, provided a due process was followed (Smith 2005, 104–5).

Technically, Buddhist monks are not to handle money themselves. It is not uncommon, therefore, to see young boys or a layman traveling with a monk for the purpose of dealing with cash transactions such as buying a bus ticket, paying a shopkeeper, or even paying for cigarettes. These boys usually handle the cash for all money transactions on behalf of the monk.

## Merit: Temples and Riches

Nevertheless, many ornate Buddhist temples and monasteries are impressively rich and beautiful beyond measure. This is often in stark contrast to the squalor of the poor and disadvantaged in surrounding villages and towns. Generally, rural village temples are more austere and simple, though there are exceptions. Much of this opulence comes from wealthy sponsors, lay donations of funds, and volunteer labor. Some abbots over certain temples have become rich and famous from their special services and giftedness, particularly through astrological forecasts and fortune telling. Some monks also use unique gifts in healing and even casting out demonic forces and unfriendly spirits. While living in Bangkok, I read a newspaper report of one monk in the capital who, daily about midafternoon, would be possessed by a green spirit, claiming to be the spirit of Jesus. Under this lying spirit's influence, the monk dispensed miraculous healings to devotees.

Japanese families install expensive Buddhist altars in their homes, often worth tens of thousands of dollars. In these *butsadan* they also place their ancestral tablets. Daily prayers and offerings are generally made before these altars. In Buddhism hundreds of ways of making merit to counter karma exist, all calculated to gain or transfer merit. Mahayana Buddhists, such as the Chinese, frequently burn paper replicas of money, cars, and mansions to send on to the deceased and to ancestors. Generally Buddhists, rich and poor alike, using their own resources, give to the Sangha and to the monks, their temples, and monasteries. This giving is not reciprocated from the monks' side. That would negate any merit being made.

## ROLES OF INTERCULTURAL WORKERS AND MONEY

Cultural anthropologists, like Paul G. Hiebert, studied much about roles and their relationships, expectations, and obligations, as they operate in family and society (1983, 139–203). The complexity of status and roles lays the foundation for an intricate set of interactions between people of different levels and positions. These tie society together.

### Missionary Lifestyles and Local Perceptions

The roles outsiders play need careful thought. Asians generally view Caucasian missionaries through glasses tinted by their stereotype of Westerners—namely white, American, Christian, and rich. Unfortunately, some expatriates reinforce that view by their lifestyles overseas, living at standards equivalent to their affluent homelands. A few refuse to eat any local cuisine, feeding only on foreign foods. Like rich business people, they live in securely guarded palatial housing, are driven in chauffeured limousines, and maintain membership in expensive, exclusive clubs on the field. While most missionaries are not in this category, their habitual living conditions are not always near the level of the people they come to serve. Their mission centers and guest houses are often set apart from local domiciles, exhibiting affluent and higher living. This raises some serious questions. Do such situations contribute barriers to effective relations and counter sensitive communication with the common local person? Furthermore, how can local

Christians possibly replicate such conditions without obtaining outside resources? How do these affect local churches?

While some local people are obviously wealthy, they may become oblivious to the needs of the poor around them. Missionaries are not to be associated with this attitude of the privileged class. They must recognize that the safety net of economic security can gradually make local needs invisible. Missionaries must especially recognize the many faces of poverty. They must seek to build relationships with influential citizens so as to proclaim the gospel to those in spiritual as well as economic poverty. However, the ever-present poor are usually more accessible. Therefore, expatriate missionaries must be extremely cautious in the roles they adopt in service. This becomes particularly complicated when it comes to the use of money, albeit for what missionaries understand are well-meant purposes.

## Patron Role Expectations and Obligations

Role confusion can easily arise where the patron decides to change obligations as perceived by the recipients of money. During our third missionary term I had an administrative role, and my wife was supervisor of the Language and Orientation Center for new missionary recruits. One of our co-workers employed a young Thai woman we hired to help her in the home. In typical Christian Western fashion this missionary decided that equality in all things was a proper value that should be exhibited in all cultures. In the spirit of compassion she decided to change some of the helper's expectations within Thai culture. She had the house help sit at the dining table and eat meals simultaneously with her and sometimes with guests. In most Thai families tradition dictates that the men eat first with their friends or guests—usually in the main room. The women and children only eat after the men are finished, and usually in the kitchen. Under this change of order, the Thai helper became confused and was soon showing disrespect to this woman missionary. The foreign co-worker was close to a breakdown. In the end, as things got more out of control, we had to let the Thai helper go.

Our analysis of this awkward problem was that, if the Thai worker served in a normal Thai household of relatives, she would be treated basically as a slave of the family. She would know their expectations and would respect the relatives' authority. She would have little freedom. She understood her role and consequently would comply, despite the bad treatment she would get. When the missionary hired her, she provided a fair wage, considerably above what would be expected in the marketplace or if she were a servant for her relatives' household. That was appropriate in an employer/employee paired relationship. But when she sat at the table to eat with her employer, the head of the household, she was out of her element and became disoriented, so much so that she acted badly towards her employer. Role confusion had produced serious role conflict. This kind of problem easily arises where the local culture is not understood and appreciated by the missionary, or where changes in role obligations and order are unwisely implemented. Conflicting roles and expectations between employer and employee, or patron and client, can easily cause significant disruption and misunderstanding.

Another aspect involved in a patron role is the issue of role sincerity. This is built around perceptions of expectations and obligations, particularly in recipients of money or assistance. As an expat, I realized that on the field I did not have the consistent resources or the guarantee of long-term local residency to function honestly in a patron role. An elderly single missionary with a generous heart had loaned money to a struggling leprosy family of believers to buy feed for the ducks they raised in the summer. The funds were to be repaid. For quite a few years the missionary continued loaning more money without getting any repayments. Then suddenly she was killed in an auto accident. The following summer the family head came to me asking for a loan. He explained his need for money to buy food for the ducks as usual. I listened and discussed this money matter with him carefully. I explained that I was not in a position to be a regular patron and did not want him to feel I was insincere in that role when I might not able to fulfill his expectation later. He seemed to understand. I did not give him the additional loan and was able to break the dependency cycle. He found a new patron elsewhere.

A Thai lawyer friend taught me a great lesson about giving. One day a well-known opium addict, a native to our province in central Thailand, visited us. He had traveled from north to central Thailand and showed me photos of other missionaries in provinces all along the way who had "baptized" him, one after the other, each of whom had reputedly given him money to help him travel down to see his father living south of us. He asked me for money to buy the bus ticket (but not rebaptism). Local believers knew him and his reputation and had warned me not to give this con man money.

In order to get some further guidance, I took him to visit my Thai lawyer friend since the addict said he knew him. My friend was also the provincial representative for his native region. During the visit I listened and learned that the opium addict had been a former student of my friend, when he had been a teacher years before. I asked him if we should give money to this man. He replied that he felt a cultural obligation to help the man in some way, not only because of the lifelong teacher/pupil relationship but especially because my friend knew his father who was the education minister for that area.

Roles, relationships, cultural obligations, and personal expectations play important functions in deciding whether to give, how much to give, and when to give or not. Western cultures tend to lack many of these obligations prevalent in the Buddhist world. Missionaries are stewards who must be clearly acquainted with these dynamics before distributing funds indiscriminately. Those who consider using patron roles need to exercise much thought and study before launching into their patron functions. Otherwise they may be criticized as becoming insincere in that role later when they leave or their positions change, thus demoralizing their network of relationships and themselves.

## The Problem of Dependency

Two sides contribute to the development of unhealthy dependency relationships in mission: first, the well-meaning individual (expatriate or national) with access to resources; and second, locals who have somehow been culturally conditioned to perceive their own economic situation as incapable of operating Christian programs (ministry) they might not otherwise consider doing and therefore have a right or an obligation to seek assistance from the most available source(s). Researchers speak of social capital whereby linking, bonding, bridging, and conditioning occur within groups. A similar process can apply when economic relationships overlap into missions. Initial contact between local believers with the enthusiastic new missionary (linking) facilitates relational connection (bridging), producing ministry cohesion (bonding), often leading to dependency (conditioning).

Sadly it is not uncommon for local Christian workers in Asia and other continents to expect funding from the West for almost everything. Many missionaries fail to recognize that a long history of Western-initiated dependency in missions has preceded them. Some local Christian leaders regularly raise monies simultaneously from several foreign agencies or individuals, reporting to all of them the same results, activities, and progress. Roger Hedlund suggests that the West provides "a happy hunting ground for a number of 'fortune hunters' from less developed countries," who sometimes "are little more than private enterprises for raising money for the promoter and his family." Conversely, Asia has become "a happy hunting ground for paternalistic Westerners who become instant experts" (1990, 275). Majority world missionaries like those from Korea and Singapore, or anyone having available resources face this same problem of subtle or straightforward dependency.

Paternalism frequently accompanies dependence. Dependency often indicates dominance of the sending culture over the mission process. The dominating outsider possesses superior knowledge, experience, and skills. This produces social inequality and a desire to execute control and authority, without giving local leaders equal rights and responsibility. This is the opposite of encouraging local indigenous control. Generally the one who handles the money defines the vision, controls the operations, and maintains the power—even in missions.

Rick Wood wrote a most enlightening article on dealing with the causes of and the cure for dependency. For its main content he interviewed Steve Saint, son of one of the five men martyred in Ecuador in 1956. Steve is currently helping the Waorani "break free from the stifling dependency created by outsiders which threatens their survival as a people" (Wood 1998, 8). This article is worth serious reading, analysis, and application.

## Money and Indigenous Church Principles

A precise definition of the term "indigenous" is: growing naturally in a region or country, being native as a plant of the soil, local as a unique animal or thing in that locality. Today, terms like "local," "contextual," and "insider" often replace "indigenous." But "local" may digress from this full connotation; "contextual" is often an outsider's attempt to enculturalize; "insider," though closer, is tainted with hints of the spy or subversive mole. Depending on who is using it, the term "indigenous" avoids negative discrimination. On the basis of definition, I prefer it. Glenn Schwartz writes, "An indigenous church should look and sound like the society of which it is a part ... not stand out as something culturally different or foreign ... concerned to carry out God's priorities in their communities" (2007, 169). "There is a direct correlation between money freely given from the West and the lack of indigeneity among the recipients ... [A seeming pipeline of money causes them] to view their churches as belonging to their 'providers' rather than as a means to give and share" (Johnson 2010, 1–2).

## Principles for Guidance

William Carey (1761–1834) conceptually followed principles for indigenous churches, Henry Venn (1796–1873) suggested the definition of the Three Selfs,

Rufus Anderson (1796–1880) endorsed them, while John Nevius (1829–1893) and Roland Allen (1868–1947) refined and emphasized them. One crucial issue Nevius and Allen raised was local rather than foreign control (a sad legacy from the colonial era). Nevius especially called for the need to be self-supporting as well as self-governing and self-propagating.

In the 1970s Alan Tippett (1911–1988) broadened the dynamics of "indigenous" (1973, 148–63) to include the local church's self-image in its community, seeing "itself as *the* Church of Jesus Christ in its own local situation, mediating the work, the mind, the word and the ministry of Christ in its own environment" (ibid., 155). It must include self-functioning and self-giving, not only for its own affairs, but also for local service projects and "the social problems of its environment." He warns: "This can be hindered by overseas funding of the home Church or board," which may stifle the initiative of the young church (ibid., 157). Tippett summarizes his indigenous concept:

> [These are] the marks of an indigenous Church when the young Church undertakes them of its own volition, when they are spontaneously done, by indigenes and within their own pattern of life. When the indigenous people of a community think of the Lord as their own, not a foreign Christ; when they do things as unto the Lord meeting the cultural needs around them, worshipping in patterns they understand; when their congregations function in participation in a body, which is structurally indigenous; then you have an indigenous Church. (ibid., 158)

No less than this is the kind of church-multiplying movement we endorse.

## Practical Funding Struggles for Consideration

When starting locally rooted work with a goal of depending on local resources, missionaries easily produce problems if we give liberally without thinking. Wisdom is required, not just thoughtless handouts. For example, in much of the Buddhist world expatriates generally have more financial resources, but are not necessarily permanent. They may be around for three or four years. Therefore, in a pioneer church-developing situation, would missionaries be wiser to give offerings equivalent to the average church member (or maybe a bit more)? Generous giving from the missionary might so distort the local finances that once the expatriates leave, a financial meltdown is likely, to the detriment of the local church.

What approach is best in order to guard against dependence or codependence which frustrates local financial responsibility? This is a dilemma we face. The remaining portion of missionary tithes and giving may be placed in a general fund for outreach or other developing church plants at the discretion of local leaders.

Other areas of consideration include pastoral salaries and construction of church buildings. Given the priesthood of all believers, are unpaid lay workers more appropriate for the body than paid pastors? Are separate church buildings and their maintenance necessary, or are house fellowships adequate? Who pays for these is important. Ideally local resources are best used from the beginning, rather than starting down the road to dependency on outside funds from the outset.

## Training National Churches in Money Matters

Churches in Buddhist communities need training in stewardship and accountability along with an easily understood system of practical bookkeeping. Teaching on ethics and organizational responsibility for recording and reporting to the members would help.

Buddhism teaches giving from one's own resources. Why should not converts be expected and taught to do the same? Certainly Christian liberality is truly free since no merit is demanded under God's grace. Why then do some new believers become spoiled and dependent on outside purses? This does not have to be.

One frequent weakness in Asia relates to misuse or misappropriation of funds, even in local churches and missions. A clear, responsible process is needed for dealing righteously but lovingly with breaches, including the culprit's redress, appropriate discipline, and spiritual restoration. Delegation of treasury duties requires responsibility, accountability, and adequate reporting to leaders, congregations, and appropriate donors. Foreign contributors should also require this reporting, rather than just give funds without expectation or accountability. Some say this can't be accomplished.

An interesting, positive example over the recent decades is China's house-church movement. Sprouting like mushrooms after rain showers, Chinese house churches have multiplied under adverse oppression, active persecution, and lack of freedom. Since 1950 the most populous nation on earth has experienced hundredfold growth in numbers of believers, many in poor rural areas. Under trying circumstances it seemed unlikely that China's churches could be self-sustaining or self-supporting. But their evangelism, church planting, leader training, pastoral growth, and missions have survived and even expanded without dependence on foreign resources. The Chinese delegation selected to attend the Third Lausanne World Congress on Evangelization, held at Cape Town in October 2010, comprised 230 delegates. Surprisingly the Chinese raised local funds sufficient to cover all their expenses to attend, plus more to cover the expenses of dozens of believers from neighboring countries. Unfortunately a backlash from the Chinese government detained and stopped all but two of the delegates from leaving the country for South Africa.

## PRACTICAL APPLICATIONS

How can Christian agencies, assemblies, and academia establish and propagate principles and policies that will help avoid and/or overcome the problem of dependency on outside funding in local missionary churches? Certainly missionaries from both the West and the majority world are to be good role models in the midst of locally run congregations, especially in restraining the overdependence upon outside funds. Keep in mind the goal for believers to transform their communities through giving themselves to reach out beyond their assemblies in evangelism, church multiplication, and community service. Outsiders need to be careful to adopt roles that will guard the selfhood, dignity, identity, control, and personal ownership of the local church and not detract the indigenous body from its true mission. Help stimulate and motivate the initiative and self-giving of the body to their community and marketplace.

Of highest importance for everyone is to depend on God for everything, including funding. "Have faith in God" was Hudson Taylor's motto for relying on the Lord to provide the mission's monies, without making personal pleas for funds. "God's work done in God's way will not lack God's supply." I remember how strengthening it was personally when by prayer alone I experienced this. Years ago, God amazingly provided this penniless student in a foreign land with money needed to buy supplies, to cover tuition, to purchase tickets to travel for family emergencies, or to buy essential clothing—all without asking human agents. Local churches and leaders can trust God for his adequate provision. Missionaries can pray and rely on God to provide for the local indigenous churches too.

Wise missionaries and established local Christians should analyze together and understand the cultural dynamics in which they serve. They must also comprehend appropriate roles to adopt within their dynamic societal ethos. Sometimes established believers become so engrossed within the church that they are isolated from the community and need to reevaluate the values, presuppositions, and practices of the milieu in which they live. When local churches act as truly indigenous ones and utilize their own resources to evangelize and transform their communities, only then will Christianity become local and normative in their cultures.

A crucial objective is to establish truly indigenous churches from the start or, if necessary, wean already established congregations from dependence on foreign funds. Changing the perceptions of local churches and their communities will foster acceptance of the idea that being a Christian does not require the denial of one's ethnic and cultural identity. Any ethnic people can be true believers without either forsaking their cultural heritage or becoming foreigners with access to money trails.

Being independent from outside finances is a bold stand that pays high dividends. Though it may seem difficult to attain, it is also satisfying and affirming. This builds strong character, personal efficiency, and spiritual stamina. Look at tasks as simple and doable through personal resources with some extension of faith. Using local funds gives significant meaning to believers and their own self-image. Spending our own money makes it *our* work and brings more meaningful value to our work. Using local funds produces pride, dignity, and self-reliance.

As much as possible, mobilize and utilize unpaid laypeople in the whole process and action, rather than depend on paid leaders, evangelists, teachers, or spiritual professionals. John Nevius declared that taking a local believer outside of his community and hiring him to do God's work immediately cuts the value of his influence in half (1958, 22). Keep him or her local, serving unpaid. Paid servants of the church supplement not supplant the local lay witness. While they may be required for certain roles, they will function as the exceptions, not the rule, since the priesthood belongs to all believers, not a few.

Finally, live within your means and existing resources. Do not go into debt. Budget and plan the uses of your money and means. Do not plan for or predict deficit budgets. The only exceptions to going into temporary debt may be when in dire, critical life-and-death emergencies or where natural disasters suddenly descend on communities. God can be trusted. Let us depend on God for the needed local resources. It is time to discard the old, colonial dependent mentality, to determine freedom from foreign funding and control, and to become fiscally independent through full reliance on God.

Being financially independent in whatever level of society one lives fully frees and empowers the local indigenous churches to grow, serve, and multiply throughout their communities. Being empathetic to the needs that surround them, wise in discerning how to respond responsibly, and generous in giving of themselves in service will have strong, positive effects on the community, more than cold handouts that cause people to feel pitied, patronized, or put down.

## REFERENCES

Bendern, Paul de, and Jul Chakravorty. 2010. New corruption scandal deals blow to India's image. November 25. Yahoo News. http://news.yahoo.com/s/nm/20101125/ts_nm/us_india_corruption (accessed November 25, 2010).

Hare, E. M., trans. 2006. *The book of the gradual sayings (Anguttara-nikaya)*. Vol. 3. Delhi: Motilal Banarsidass.

Hedlund, Roger E. 1990. Cheaper by the dozen? Indigenous missionaries vs. partnership. *Evangelical Missions Quarterly* 26, no. 3 (July): 274–79.

Hiebert, Paul G. 1983. *Cultural anthropology*. Grand Rapids: Baker Book House.

Johnson, Jean. 2010. Cultural identity and new found faith. *WMA Perspectives*, August–September. http://www.wmausa.org/files/Documents/WMA%20Docs/AugustSeptember%202010%20Newsletter%20Revised.pdf.

Nevius, John L. 1958. *The planting and development of missionary churches*. Philadelphia: Reformed and Presbyterian Publishing.

*Newsweek.* April 5, 2009.

Schwartz, Glenn J. 2007. *When charity destroys dignity*. Lancaster, PA: World Mission Associates.

Smith, Alex G. 2005. Transfer of merit in folk Buddhism. In *Sharing Jesus holistically with the Buddhist world*, eds. David Lim and Steve Spaulding, 99–124. Pasadena: William Carey Library.

Tippett, Alan R. 1973. *Verdict theology in missionary theory*. Pasadena: William Carey Library.

Wood, Rick. 1998. Fighting dependency among the Aucas: An interview with Steve Saint. *Mission Frontiers*, May–June. http://www.missionfrontiers.org/issue/article/fighting-dependency-among-the-aucas.

Woodward, F. L., trans. 2005. *The book of the kindred sayings (Samyutta-Nikaya)*. Part 5. Delhi: Motilal Banarsidass.

# 3

# MONEY AND MISSIONARY LIFESTYLE IN THE BUDDHIST WORLD

## Andrew Thomas

What is the impact of the financial lifestyle of missionaries upon people with a Buddhist worldview? How does this impact the way the gospel is communicated? As a missionary myself, I would like to suggest that the impact of Christian ministry in the Buddhist world hinges on the way money is viewed and used by Western missionaries working in the Buddhist world. I write as a missionary living in the Buddhist world and married to a Cambodian believer.

This is a very challenging topic, as earning, spending, and giving money are all activities which are not merely mechanical, they are an expression of one's worldview and value system. When one spends, gives, or earns money, one is expressing one's core being and showing other people what it is that one holds dear. Money usage can also be both a cause and a result of character development. More importantly, one's use of money has an impact on the lives of others—those who receive money from us and those who observe our use of it. This paper will examine the guiding principles all Christians should apply when using money. More specifically, this paper will ask whether Western Christian missionaries should live at a financial level above their target audience, below them, or equal to them in the light of strategic missional results in the Buddhist world.

## PRINCIPLES OF USING MONEY

Some basic, underlying principles of using money in ministry are clear for all believers but difficult to apply. We can safely say the central principle is love. This was confirmed by Jesus in his teaching:

> One of them, an expert in the law, tested him with this question: "Teacher, which is the greatest commandment in the Law?" Jesus replied: "'Love the Lord your God with all your heart and with all your soul and with all your mind.' This is the first and greatest commandment. And the second is like it: 'Love your neighbor as yourself.' All the Law and the Prophets hang on these two commandments." (Matt 22:35–40)

Therefore love should be the guiding principle of all Christians, including Western missionaries. This includes the use of money. Missionary spending, saving, and giving patterns should not contradict this. This means missionaries should carefully consider the consequences—especially in the long term—of spending, giving, and saving. Missionaries should ask whether people will truly be helped in this life—by examining them over a period of five years—and in the next life. We must examine whether our use of money will bring lasting good and bear spiritual fruit, bringing people closer to heaven, God, and righteousness, and far from sin and evil. Here we are not talking about ignoring temporal needs, but rather prioritizing spiritual needs. When missionaries spend disproportionately large amounts of money on schooling, medical care, and entertainment, this seems to be setting a trend for national believers to follow. They will aspire to the missionary lifestyle and may miss the most important essence of the message.

The principle of valuing people above money is also an important one. Jesus said a person's soul is more important than the whole world, by saying it didn't make sense to gain the whole world by losing one's self (Luke 9:25). People are more important than things. Therefore missionaries should be prepared to spend even large amounts of money and work with all of their might to see people come to faith in Christ; this should be done without focusing on the cost. When interacting with unbelievers, one should always be alert for opportunities to share Christ (Eph 5:16). This can be hindered by conflict that arises over finances. For example, when a local merchant tries to exploit one as a foreigner, one should approach this graciously and not jeopardize a precious ministry opportunity. Perhaps it would be best to confront the merchant in a friendly manner without becoming annoyed or scolding him or her. This requires wisdom. B. J. Thomas once sang that one should use things and love people rather than love things and use people (1979, track 1). This seems to be good advice and shows us that people, because they are supremely valuable, are to be loved, not used. Money, because of its inferior nature, is to be used, not loved.

An example of this occurs (far too regularly) when a Western missionary is involved in a car accident with a poor person and the missionary is not at fault. When this happens, the missionary can insist upon receiving payment from the other and can go to extreme measures to extract the money, even using expensive lawyers in the process. Or the missionary can choose to forgive the debt and use this as an opportunity to illustrate how God forgave the great debt of sin that we owe. This is bringing the use of money into the ministry lifestyle of the missionary.

## INCARNATIONAL MINISTRY AND SERVANTHOOD

With regard to the social class or financial level of Christians, incarnational ministry as exemplified by both Christ and the Apostle Paul emphasizes the need for missionaries to become like those among whom they are privileged to serve. It also emphasizes servanthood. Missionaries should thus seek to follow Paul and Christ's example as far as possible.

> Though I am free and belong to no one, I have made myself a slave to everyone, to win as many as possible. To the Jews I became like a Jew, to win the Jews. To those under the law I became like one under the law (though I myself am not under the law), so as to win those under the law. To those not having the law I became like one not having the law (though I am not free from God's law but am under Christ's law), so as to win those not having the law. To the weak I became weak, to win the weak. I have become all things to all people so that by all possible means I might save some. (1 Cor 9:19–22)

Servanthood would suggest that a practice of using missionary funds to employ national Christians with the expectation that they be subservient is flawed and contrary to true servanthood. Nevertheless this is a very common, popular practice. Missionary organizations fill the upper levels of leadership with volunteer expatriates and have locals performing local tasks. To many, this is so normal that it's impossible to conceive of ministry done any other way.

Having missionaries in senior positions does little to empower locals. A ministry that adopts an approach like this will either be perpetually dependent on foreign input and incoming staff or will collapse when missionaries withdraw. In addition, staff will often work in order to obtain a salary without taking ownership. If missionaries enter as servants, they can serve as forerunners to a movement of national believers by supporting and encouraging locals to follow their own visions, perceptions of need, and concepts of ministry. John the Baptist said it was necessary for him to decrease in order for Jesus to increase (John 3:30). Jesus himself said that we could do greater miracles than he did (John 14:12). Therefore missionaries should use funds to empower national believers and not enslave or control them.

## IDENTIFICATION

The principle of identification dictates that one has to be like one's audience; identification enables our audience to think that they can attain what we have attained. As Jesus entered fully into our level of living and working, we as missionaries are also to fully enter into and work at the level of others so they can relate to us. If we are too comfortable, they will think our success is related to our comfort or resources and pursue them rather than a relationship with God.

In the village where I live, it is possible for a missionary to live in a house similar to those of local people. When one is sick one can—sometimes with difficulty—find a local doctor for treatment. One can have one's children educated in a local school, travel by motorbike and bicycle, and live in a house that opens onto the street. This is an inexpensive option. The other option for foreigners is to live aloof by driving an expensive car and living in a gated community where one is secluded from one's neighbors. This is an expensive, detached lifestyle. Though missionaries may possess significant wealth in their home country, this is not to be grasped at.

In your relationships with one another, have the same mindset as Christ Jesus: Who, being in very nature God, did not consider equality with God something to be used to his own advantage; rather, he made himself nothing by taking the very nature of a servant, being made in human likeness. And being found in appearance as a man, he humbled himself by becoming obedient to death—even death on a cross! Therefore God exalted him to the highest place and gave him the name that is above every name, that at the name of Jesus every knee should bow, in heaven and on earth and under the earth. (Phil 2:5–10)

As missionaries we should adopt an obedient, submissive lifestyle, forgetting the financial privileges or social standing to which we felt entitled back home. We should be willing to be ridiculed—as may happen in language acquisition or when others see our foreign ways—and be willing to suffer deprivation of comforts or things that make us feel safe, such as Western medical facilities, comfortable accommodation, and high standards of living. Jesus became like us in every way so that we can be like him.

For surely it is not angels he helps, but Abraham's descendants. For this reason he had to be made like them, fully human in every way, in order that he might become a merciful and faithful high priest in service to God, and that he might make atonement for the sins of the people. Because he himself suffered when he was tempted, he is able to help those who are being tempted. (Heb 2:16–18)

By this measure it would seem appropriate for missionaries to adopt a lifestyle similar to local people. This is a radical approach, unpalatable and seemingly impractical to many. It would seem inappropriate to some to educate one's children in local schools because local schools have educational standards lower than those to which one is accustomed at home. Local hospitals are sometimes unsanitary. Public transportation is uncomfortable, and neighborhoods may be noisy, unhealthy, dirty, or crime ridden. One wants to have one's technological gadgets on hand at all times for ease of communication. When considering this matter, these questions arise: Did our heavenly Father insure that his Son was born in a sanitary hospital (or contemporary equivalent in Israel)? Did God send his Son to study in the best seminary and shield him from manual labor? At the penultimate act, did God insure his Son die with dignity in a comfortable environment surrounded only by loving well-wishers and supporters? We know the answers to these questions, but the implications are painfully difficult for many to implement.

The result is that many missionaries live at a financial level largely unattainable by national believers. Their modes of transport, education, and medical care have created a relational barrier by which missionaries are segregated from the wider society. This may result in the error Alex Smith warned about when he wrote,

"The church must be kept from becoming an insular subsociety which fails to communicate Christ effectively to its Buddhist neighbors" (1978, 1).

Often Buddhists are seen as promoting monasticism (with a vow of poverty) and equating it with holiness; however, this view is changing. Recently Buddhists are seeing the value of abandoning monasticism. In India, Ambedkar warned new Buddhists that the committed should remain in contact with the common people, rather than becoming isolated in monastic centers and dependent on patronage. He envisaged a new kind of Buddhist worker, one who would function within society and help to affect a transformation of society (Friends of the Western Buddhist Order 2010, 1).

What are the missiological implications? Christians should live, walk, and work among the people to whom they are called to minister. The concept of a secluded missionary compound or center must be abandoned.

By becoming like us, Jesus showed that godliness and spiritual power can be attained within the confines of a human body and the rigor of day-to-day life. In his final act of glorification where he ascended to the right hand of the Father, he showed us the wonderful consequences of such humility, a divine example of delayed gratification. This is expressed well by Thomas and Elizabeth Brewster in their article entitled "Bonding and the Missionary Task", "Jesus left heaven where he belonged and became a belonger with humankind in order to draw people into a belonging relationship with God" (1982, 3). The Brewsters advise missionaries to live simply: to be willing to live with a local family, limit personal belongings to twenty kilograms, use only public transportation, and expect to carry out language learning in the context of relationships that the learner is responsible for developing and maintaining (ibid., 9).

Another side benefit of adopting the local people's lifestyle in poor countries is that it reduces expenses so the expatriate's supporters will be able to support more missionaries and other ministries. In addition, it means missionaries will not have to raise extremely large sums of money for subsistence. For example, Hudson Taylor adopted much of the local dress and culture when he went to the mission field. Ed Reese, his biographer, said of him after he was robbed in 1856, "With no salary coming in now he would have been destitute and helpless had not his expenses fallen sharply because he had adopted the Chinese dress and level of living" (n.d.). Paul sought to remove anything from himself that would distract people from the power of God. He was concerned that even his eloquence of speech might do that (1 Cor 2:4,5). Most expatriate missionaries attempting to speak the languages found in the Buddhist world have little to fear in that regard.

It seems that national believers may be distracted by the wealth of missionaries in the same way. Our relatively great wealth could persuade them to put their trust in wealth and not in God. The fact that many national believers forsake the work of God and pursue wealth or become hirelings in Christian organizations, working for a salary with motives mercenary and not honorable may in fact be linked to this distraction. They aspire to be as the missionaries are—with all their possessions and foreign comforts—and this leads them to an unhealthy focus on wealth. They follow the pattern mentioned by Paul as a warning to Timothy:

> Those who want to get rich fall into temptation and a trap and into many foolish and harmful desires that plunge people into ruin and destruction. For the love of money is a root of all kinds of evil. Some people, eager for money, have wandered from the faith and pierced themselves with many griefs. (1 Tim 6:9,10)

Incidentally, this warning against covetousness concurs with Buddhist doctrine. In "Aquinas and Dogen on Poverty and the Religious Life," Douglas K. Mikkelson quotes the Zen master Dōgen:

> Monks should take care to follow the conduct of the Buddhas and the Patriarchs. Above all, do not covet wealth. It is impossible to put into words the depth of the Tathagata's compassion. Everything he did was for the sake of all sentient beings. (2006, 3)

So abhorrence for covetousness is an important point of agreement between Buddhists and Christians. We should therefore insure that our lifestyle bears testimony to this abhorrence and not the materialistic philosophy of Wallace Wattles, who said:

> It is not possible to live a really complete or successful life unless one is rich. No one can rise to his greatest possible height in talent or soul development unless he has plenty of money, for to unfold the soul and to develop talent he must have many things to use, and he cannot have these things unless he has money to buy them with. (1996, 9)

While this philosophy is blatantly and unashamedly materialistic and raises feelings of disgust in many, it would seem that some missionaries, seemingly unconsciously, practice this doctrine by their lifestyles while vehemently denying with their words that they believe in it. However, this brings to mind the words of Jesus who said, "Watch out! Be on your guard against all kinds of greed; life does not consist in an abundance of possessions" (Luke 12:15). A lifestyle of identification clearly confirms Jesus' doctrine and illustrates that spirituality and success is accessible to normal people in daily life even when economic resources are limited.

## IDENTIFICATION CAN INVITE SCORN

It is valuable to note, however, that it is not essential to live at an extremely low economic level in order to be effective. The aim is to be at the same level as others. It has been my experience, married to a Cambodian, that some of my humble habits (for example, drinking coffee in a modest—it would seem cheap—coffee shop) have invited the scorn of my wife's family. This is best understood in the context of a Buddhist worldview. My poverty (as they perceive it) is seen to be as a result of wrongdoing in a previous life. Alfred Bloom, in *Understanding Karma and Transmigration in Buddhism*, says:

> Karma assumes the ultimate justice of life. The punishment always fits the crime. The conditions of one's birth into this world and the succeeding developments in one's life are seen as the result of one's decisions and actions in previous lives. Karma and Transmigration explained the birth of disabled people, prodigies, or one's status in life, high or low, such as the economic or social class one is born into. (n.d.)

Therefore, in the eyes of Buddhist family and friends, my lowly status today indicates I am suffering as a result of sin in a past life and am therefore worthy of their scorn. The question arises as to what the strategic significance of a humble lifestyle is for effectiveness as a missionary. It would seem that one should be living at a level similar to those one wants to reach with the gospel, even if this results in being an object of scorn, both by the rich and the economically challenged. For a missionary to be effective in, for example, many affluent Japanese or Korean contexts, living a life similar to that of a poor person would probably have little or no positive impact.

For many in a Western environment, living at a level equal to one's target audience is a challenge, especially when it impinges on our preferences, comfort, hygiene, or sense of self-respect. Missionaries may fear disease or accidents because of a lack of emergency financial resources, such as medical insurance. It is interesting to note that some missionary organizations and ministries insist on medical coverage, costing several thousands of dollars, as a prerequisite for missionary service. The reasons for this are understandable but may in effect make missionary service prohibitively expensive.

## THE PRACTICE OF GIVING

What about the practice of giving? This opens a whole host of complex possibilities. Every act of giving is unique and controversial, depending on the viewpoint of the giver, the recipient, and the observer. Christ is clear in his teaching on giving to the poor, and a clear practice of his teaching is likely to meet with the approval of Buddhists. Thus it seems that Christians should be active in giving in order to let their light of testimony shine to their Buddhist neighbors. Christ said we should give or lend things to people who ask us for something (Matt 5:42). Old Testament teaching calls giving to the poor lending to the Lord, and says the Lord will repay us (Prov 19:17).

In Buddhism, generosity is also seen as central. Jacqueline Kramer, in *Generosity in Buddhism*, says the following:

> Many westerners believe that the practice of meditation is the basis of Buddhist practice. But Buddhism is much richer and more multilayered than that. Generosity was the first practice the Buddha taught to lay people when he travelled throughout India. If spiritual practitioners are well grounded in generosity; their hearts are more available for insight when they sit down to meditate. Because Buddhists place great importance on generosity they have many words to describe it, just as the Eskimos have many words for snow. Two of these words are *Dana* and *Caga*. *Dana* translates as "distribution of gifts." *Caga* translates as "a heart bent on giving." *Dana*, or giving, is intimately tied to karma, or cause and effect. *Caga* describes the state of mind of the generous giver, or the desire to give. It is *Caga* that creates a rich soil for our meditation. (n.d.)

Yet it will be apparent to observers that while Buddhists and Christians agree that giving is important, Buddhist giving has no tangible, immediate results—

though it promises spiritual advancement. Those who give live and die in poverty enjoying the modest privilege of visiting lavishly decorated pagodas—decorated with the aid of their donations.

Christians can use the Buddhist concept of giving as a "bridge" enabling them to establish a point of agreement after which one can illuminate the differences. This is especially interesting when one reads the following:

> There are three degrees of generosity spoken of in Buddhism. The first degree is miserly giving. This is when we give away that which we no longer want. It is considered miserly because giving in this way asks nothing of us. This sort of giving is like recycling, and it is valuable but not particularly generous. The next level of generosity is kindly giving. With kindly giving we give away what we would like to receive. There is a thoughtfulness and friendliness in this kind of giving. The third, and highest, form of giving is kingly giving. In kingly giving we give the very best of what we have in time, material goods, or, in some cases, even our lives. (ibid.)

Jesus practiced kingly giving—he gave his life for us. God loves a cheerful giver (2 Cor 9:7) and not a miserly giver. In general Buddhists—if they see Christians succeeding by giving yet abounding, according to Proverbs 11:24 and 2 Corinthians 9:7–9—will realize the inadequacy of their worldview and realize the validity of the gospel.

> Many Buddhists who have come to Christ have first come "to the end of themselves." Many conversions from Buddhism swing on the pivot point of the inability to accomplish perfection by oneself. (Smith 1978, 11)

## DEPENDENCY AND TRUSTING IN HUMANS

What is not immediately clear, however, is how to respond to the negative aspect of giving, where it leads to dependency. Dependency is not merely a distasteful state of affairs which offends our sense of human dignity and individual responsibility. In *A Vision of Global Communion*, Mesach Krisetya says of dependency, "Theologically speaking, a relationship of dependency is totally wrong also because the orientation is to self: self-existence, self-survival, self-prestige" (2001, 62). It seems to be a spiritual problem, based on selfishness. Dependency focuses on what others can do for oneself. It also may stem from trusting in humans as opposed to God. Thirdly, it may stem from laziness and an unwillingness to take responsibility for one's own subsistence.

Paul sought to set an example by earning his living and not depending on his flock; he did this to be an example to them.

> For you yourselves know how you ought to follow our example. We were not idle when we were with you, nor did we eat anyone's food without paying for it. On the contrary, we worked night and day, laboring and toiling so that we would not be a burden to any of you. We did this, not because we do not have the right to such help, but in order to offer ourselves as a model for you to imitate. For even when we were with you, we gave you this rule: "The one who is unwilling to work shall not eat." (2 Thess 3:7–10)

This may suggest that missionaries should all be self-supporting, providing for themselves by means of employment or enterprise of some sort. Such a life of industry in the marketplace also has the advantage of showing that vibrant living for Christ is possible in the context of what is normal for national believers. However this is not true in all cases, as Paul says, "The Lord has commanded that those who preach the gospel should receive their living from the gospel" (1 Cor 9:14). The error to which Paul was referring above was that of the lazy who do little work and depend on others for their sustenance.

Another aspect of dependency is that it often involves a shift of focus: one is no longer trusting in God, but in humans. Trusting in fellow humans is condemned by God and brings us under a curse (Jer 17:5–8). We should try to avoid any activities which encourage people to trust in missionaries—or even themselves—at the expense of trusting in God. This would cause them to stumble. What is to be said about meeting the needs of the people to whom we minister? We are to feed the hungry, clothe the naked, give a drink to the thirsty, and visit the sick and imprisoned (Matt 25:31–46). Mere platitudes or encouraging messages are not sufficient (Jas 2:15–17). However, we are also in danger of becoming so focused on physical needs that spiritual needs are neglected. As Jesus asked, "What good is it for someone to gain the whole world, and yet lose or forfeit their very self?" (Luke 9:25). There is also the danger of people coming to attend church, professing faith in Christ, and joining our organizations for the physical benefits they can receive. Glenn Schwartz, in *Is There a Cure for Dependency among Mission-established Churches?* says:

> When people come into the Christian faith for the material possessions they get—something goes terribly wrong in the spread of the Gospel. That might be the single most important reason why the dependency problem so often cripples the Christian movement and why it is so urgent that it be avoided or dealt with where it exists. (2000)

These seemingly contradictory demands and situations constitute a serious dilemma for missionaries and ministers in all situations. Conventional solutions are seldom, if ever, effective.

As one way of teaching dependence on God, missionaries can organize concentrated, focused, and persistent prayer asking God to intervene to solve the problem of poverty in their community. Glenn Schwartz, in *Searching for Meaningful Ways to Help the Poor*, tells the following story:

> The congregation decided to begin a prayer meeting for the unemployed at 5:00 pm three days a week—Monday, Wednesday and Friday. He said it was not long until people became productive in their various areas of employment—particularly the fields in which their crops were grown. These efforts were so blessed of the Lord that they soon had so much produce that it could not all be used locally. They then began to pray about ways to get the produce to markets in the capital city many kilometers away. The church put legs to their own prayers, and businessmen with big trucks donated their services to carry the extra produce to the city. How many times have we thought of a prayer meeting three times a week as a solution to the problem of poverty? (2001)

This agrees with Hudson Taylor's philosophy which says we must learn to trust God in prayer (Barlow 1976, 2) and "God's work, done God's way, will not lack God's supply" (Reese n.d.). If we as missionaries have apparently limitless financial resources, and it is perceived that we depend on them, locals will perhaps be tempted to seek wealth as an answer to their problems. However, if local believers see us as fellow strugglers on the journey of life, depending on God, they will be encouraged to depend on God too. Schwartz also promotes the idea of teaching believers how to give—not necessarily of their meager financial resources—but of their labor or produce. Great damage has been done not teaching the principle of giving.

Perhaps someday we will realize how much of the poverty of the Christian movement can be laid at the feet of those who have excused people from giving back to God even when their giving seemed small and insignificant. One woman in East Africa told how she discovered that if you give zero to God, He can multiply it and it will still be zero. She then asked what happens to a little when it is put into the hands of the One who can multiply without measure. (2001)

Another valuable way of helping local people, and at the same time maintaining their dignity, is by means of revolving loan plans. The following quote expresses it very clearly:

Resist the temptation to use your resources to do for others what they can and should do for themselves. Consider the benefits of investing in micro-enterprise development projects. In our day, development personnel are discovering the value of such things as revolving loan funds and other self-help programs. Remember, too, that the best source of such funds could well be the local community in which the funds are to be used. Some of the most successful revolving loan funds are those where the principal being lent out comes from people within the community. (Schwartz n.d.)

In Cambodia, World Vision has established the "Vision Fund" to help people to develop enterprises. The dependency issue is particularly relevant for missionaries in that it demands that we carefully consider our giving to make sure it truly helps people and does not cause them to remain trapped in poverty, trapped in laziness, or cursed because of dependence on fellow human beings.

## CONCLUSION

In the use of money by missionaries, love is a central principle, and people are always to be put before things. We should always be alert for opportunities to share Christ, even where financial loss may be incurred. Incarnational ministry and servanthood implies we should become like our target audience as far as possible. Missionaries must not be an insular subsociety. Servanthood suggests that a practice of using funds to employ national Christians with the expectation that they be subservient is unbiblical. One should seek to fill the upper levels of leadership with locals and have volunteer expatriates in servant roles. Identification helps one's audience to think that they can attain what we have attained; godliness and spiritual power can be attained within the confines of a human body and the rigor of day-to-day life. We seek intimate relationships with humankind in order to draw people into a belonging relationship with God. Buddhists are seeing the value of abandoning monasticism and will understand our closeness with the community. Living like one's audience reduces expenses and removes anything that will distract people from the power of God. Buddhism and Christianity's opposition to covetousness is an important point of agreement. We missionaries should insure that our lifestyle agrees with our doctrine. Identification sometimes invites scorn from the rich and powerful, but this is to be endured, not avoided. With regard to giving, it is controversial but Buddhists and Christians agree it is central, and it is therefore a "bridge" for ministry. Weaknesses in the Buddhist concept of giving enable missionaries to teach the truth. Giving may result in selfish or lazy dependency where people trust in man and focus on material things. We as leaders need to teach local people to trust God in prayer and encourage them to give. Where funds are needed for development and starting enterprises, revolving loan funds can be established.

All this serves to illuminate the need for self-examination to establish what hidden messages are being sent when missionaries give to others or spend money. The impact of Christian ministry in the Buddhist world hinges on the way money is viewed and used by missionaries. Therefore, missionaries should insure they are following the principles of identification, effective incarnational ministry and—tying it all together—love, which seeks the best interests of its object.

# REFERENCES

Barlow, Fred. 1976. *Profiles in evangelism*. Murfreesboro, TN: Sword of the Lord.

Brewster, E. Thomas, and Elizabeth S. Brewster. 1982. *Bonding and the missionary task*. Pasadena: Lingua House.

Cobb, John B. Jr. 2002. A Buddhist-Christian critique of neo-liberal economics. Lecture presented at the Eastern Buddhist conference, Otani University, Kyoto, Japan, May 18.

Friends of the Western Buddhist Order. 2010. Money in perspective. http://fwbo.org/articles/money_in_perspective.html.

Instilling Goodness School. 2002. Following the Buddha's footsteps. Instilling Goodness School. http://online.sfsu.edu/~rone/Buddhism/footsteps.htm.

Kramer, Jacqueline. n.d. Generosity in Buddhism. Learning to Give. http://learningtogive.org/faithgroups/voices/generosity_in_buddhism.asp.

Krisetya, Mesach. 2001. A vision of global communion. *Vision: A Journal for Church and Theology* 2, no. 1 (Spring): 59–67. http://www.mennovision.org/Vol%202%20No%201/vision2.1.pdf.

Little, Christopher. 2000. When two bikes split a church. *Mission Frontiers*, November–December. http://www.missionfrontiers.org/issue/article/when-two-bikes-split-a-church.

Mahabodhi Society of USA. 2002. How to reach financial nirvana. Mahabodhi Society of USA. http://www.mahabodhi.org/intro/financialNirvana.ppt.

Mahidol University. 2002. Buddhism. Mahidol University. http://www.mahidol.ac.th/budsir/buddhism.htm.

Mikkelson, Douglas K. 2006. Aquinas and Dogen on poverty and the religious life. *Journal of Buddhist Ethics* 13: 85–111.

Myanmar Ministry of Religious Affairs. 2003. Doing the act of charity. http://web.ukonline.co.uk/buddhism/charity.html.

Reese, Ed. n.d. Biography of Hudson Taylor. European-American Evangelistic Crusades. http://www.eaec.org/faithhallfame/hudsontaylor.htm.

Roberts, Charles F. 1999. The Salvation Army: Retooling for the post-modern world. Next-Wave. http://www.next-wave.org/apr99/SA.htm.

Sayadaw, Mahasi. n.d. The theory of karma. Buddha Dharma Education Association and BuddhaNet. http://www.buddhanet.net/e-learning/karma.htm.

Schwartz, Glenn. 2000. Is there a cure for dependency among mission-established churches? World Mission Associates. http://www.wmausa.org/page.aspx?id=83812.

———. 2001. Searching for meaningful ways to help the poor. World Mission Associates. http://www.wmausa.org/page.aspx?id=83811.

———. n.d. Developing a world Christian lifestyle. World Mission Associates. http://www.wmausa.org/page.aspx?id=189345.

Sen, Hun. 2008. Dialogue on interfaith cooperation for peace and harmony. Speech presented at the opening of a conference at the Intercontinental Hotel, Phnom Penh, April 3.

Siddhisambhava. 2009. Understanding money, understanding ourselves, and bringing money into our practice. FWBO & TBMSG News. http://www.fwbo-news.org/features/Siddhisambhava%20-%20money%20-%20bringing%20it%20into%20our%20practice.pdf.

Smith, Alex G. 1978. The gospel facing Buddhist cultures. Paper presented at the Asian Leadership Conference on Evangelization, University of Singapore, November 1–10.

Thomas, B. J. 1979. You gave me love. Myrrh Records.

Wattles, Wallace D. 1996. The science of getting rich. Santa Fe, NM: Sun Books. (Orig. pub. 1910.)

# 4

# POSSESSIONS, POSITIONS, AND POWER: MATERIAL ASYMMETRIES AND THE MISSIONARY CALL

## Jonathan J. Bonk

In his book, *Faith, Morals, and Money: What the World's Religions Tell Us about Ethics and the Marketplace*, Edward D. Zinbarg argues that the dominant ethical theme in Buddhism—whether Theravada, Mahayana, or Zen—is compassion. While the Theravadan tradition stresses patience and contentment with one's lot in life—both of which suffuse the teaching of Jesus—Mahayana sources feed on Buddhist social activism (Zinbarg 2005, 69). Buddhist and Christian theoretical understanding of what it means to live righteously, while beginning and ending in very different places, have some things in common. Both advocate altruistic compassion; both are highly critical of ostentatious materialism; both stress self-discipline and moderation as a way of life; and both understand that all things are interrelated. That is, we live in a moral universe where behavior matters.

The missional significance of social networks is well illustrated in Paul De Neui's edited volume, *Family and Faith in Asia: The Missional Impact of Social Networks* (2010). Since the relative abundance of possessions bears directly on a person's social statuses and their concomitant role expectations within these networks, the question of mission and money is of deep import socially, theologically, and therefore missiologically. If the subject of possessions were not so pervasive in the Christian Scriptures, missionaries could be forgiven for acquiescing to their culturally generated sense of material entitlement—constantly escalating since the West long ago decided that mammon is the measure of all things.

Exploration of the roots of poverty and elucidation of the supposed wellsprings of affluence were neither the purposes of my book *Missions and Money* (first published in 1991), nor are they the focus of this chapter, as important as these subjects might be (Smith 2005, xi). Nor was it or is it my intention to address the immensely complex, ideologically polarizing questions swirling around missiological debates about dependency and interdependency. Rather, my attempt was then, and is now, to show how both the effectiveness and the integrity of decent, well-meaning missionaries and mission organizations can be compromised when their theories and practices are demonstrably at odds with those of the Lord they proclaim.

The argument of this paper may be summarized as follows:

- For the past two hundred years, and especially the last fifty years, missionaries from the West have tended to be materially wealthy, relative to most people in the so-called mission fields in which a majority of them serve, and this affluence is at least partially due to factors which cannot be replicated by the poor today.

- It follows that what the Bible says to and about the rich, it says to and about Western missionaries. Wealth and poverty are among the most frequently recurring themes in our Christian Scriptures (Wallis 2000, 6–7). While gross economic inequity in close social proximity poses profound relational, communicatory, and strategic challenges for missionaries, more serious are the complex questions of ethical integrity that challenge us as wealthy followers of Jesus in contexts of profound poverty.

- Since neither missionary training nor on-field orientation adequately prepare aspiring missionaries to acknowledge or address the ethical compromises characterizing those who—in St. Paul's words—"peddle the word of God for profit" (2 Cor 2:17) in contexts of poverty, it is vital that the institutions and agencies responsible for training missionaries and facilitating mission work address the issues directly, deliberately, persistently, and biblically through training, mentoring, and policy.

# MISSIONARIES AND THE ABUNDANCE OF POSSESSIONS

When Western missionaries discover themselves to be materially wealthy, relative to most people in the so-called mission fields in which a majority of them serve, they should understand that their good fortune is at least partially due to factors which cannot be replicated by the poor today. While the statistical data informing both the first and second editions of my book is now out of date, the integrity of its central argument seems to have been reinforced in the twenty years since it first appeared. In an article published in the *International Bulletin of Missionary Research* more than twenty years ago, I noted that throughout the period often referred to as the "William Carey Era" of modern missions, the per capita gross national products of the developed and underdeveloped worlds widened from a factor of less than two to one in 1792, to three to one by 1913, and seven to one by 1970 (Bonk 1989). Since then, the situation has actually deteriorated for more than 20 percent of the world's population. According to recent World Bank figures, approximately 1.5 billion people subsist on less than one dollar per day, while some 2.8 billion live on less than two dollars per day (Smith 2005, 1–8).

Missionaries from Western lands, on the other hand, reflecting the culturally prescribed material entitlements of aggressively consumer cultures, grow ever more rich by the standards of a majority of the world's population. In an email message received on August 17, 2005, the "basic support" of a missionary family—good friends of mine who were en route to South Africa with a well-known faith mission—was pegged at $4,344 per month. An additional estimated $600 in monthly "ministry funds" would also be needed, on top of "outgoing funds" in excess of $19,000. However inadequate $60,000 per annum might be for sustaining a North American family at levels of minimal social and material entitlement in a bicultural, intercontinental ministry, it guarantees them a place among the privileged in the social hierarchy of South Africa. How easily accustomed we become to our escalating scale of material entitlements, with one generation's luxuries mutating into another generation's needs. Peter C. Whybrow observes that "as America's commercial hegemony has increased and our social networks have eroded, we have lost any meaningful reference as to how rich we really are, especially in comparison to other nations" (Whybrow 2005, 38–39).

While libraries of books have been written explaining how this fortunate state of economic affairs arose, and how—with assiduous attention to the proper economic ideology—increasing levels of consumption can continue not only forever but for everyone, Western affluence is at least partially due to factors which cannot be replicated by the poor today. In a more innocent age, it was possible for Western missionaries to believe that their relatively comfortable way of life was the inevitable outcome of a national life organized in a Christian way, and that, given enough time and sufficient conversions, the poorer peoples of the world could one day likewise enjoy the good life. Not only were Christianity and civilization inseparable but, in the sober judgment of some of the keenest Christian thinkers of that day, no one could "become a Christian in the true sense of the term, however savage [they] may have been before, without becoming ... civilized" (East 1844, 243).

Sixteen years into the twentieth century, with "civilized" nations in the throes of one of the most savage and pointless struggles in the pathetically war-strewn record of humankind, it was still bravely asserted that:

> The civilisation which is called Western is the slowly developed product of religion ... [and has] surged forward to its present high water by means of the internal pressure of its inner Christian élan, ... an impulse which is but the expression of a Christian principle of life moving within. (MacDonald 1916, 54)

Many Americans, regarding their nation as the apex of Western civilization and avatar of universal progress—the "almost chosen nation" (Shoemaker 2006)—unapologetically pursue their "manifest destiny" of political, cultural, economic, and military hegemony. But to those who look more closely at the why and how of this ascendancy, Western Christendom—born and sustained through violence—has been demystified. Obscured by the noble ideals and economic ideology to which we attribute a way of life that is the envy of the world lies a more sinister history which cannot be legitimately replicated by our would-be emulators: centuries of brutal slavery that emptied Africa of an estimated 60 million of its inhabitants; genocidal conquest of three continents that issued in the obliteration of an estimated 90 percent of their incumbent populations; a two-ocean moat and a century of relatively cheap national defense; maintenance of a privileged position through both the actual and threatened use of nuclear and chemical weapons of mass destruction; such instruments of development are not available to the poor today. While factors such as these do not mitigate the inherent economic and social advantages of a democratic way of life based on law and the protection of private property, they should at the very least induce a profound humility in those of us who consciously serve as exemplars of Christianity or development in the "underdeveloped" populations of our world. It is difficult to imagine what the lands of old Christendom would be like today if virtually the entire populations of the Americas, Australia, and New Zealand—together with large segments of South Africa and Israel—were packed into what is today known as greater Europe.

The political-economic ideology on which America places it trust and which it will defend at all costs is built on the assumption that it is entitled to perpetual economic growth, and that such growth is possible, desirable, and necessary. In the two decades following World War II, "the expectation of plenty ... became the reigning assumption of social thought" (Shi 1985, 248). The word which perhaps best sums up the plethora of secular values which influence all North Americans— including missionaries—from infancy throughout life is "consumerism," the way of life established upon the principle that the great goal of human life and activity is more things, better things, and newer things; in short, that life does consist in the abundance of possessions.

Consumerism is—to use Robert Bellah's expression—a "habit" of the heart that affects everything Americans are and do (Bellah et al. 1985). When combined with the popular equation of "progress" with technological sophistication, and "civilization" with abundance, Western consumerism makes justification of increasingly high standards of missionary living almost inevitable.

American anthropologist Jules Henry (1904–1968) noted this preoccupation with consumption in 1963 when he suggested that life in North America could be summed up by two great commandments: "Create more desire" and "Thou shalt consume" (Henry 1963, 19). American well-being, he argued, rested on the faithful obedience of the majority to these two imperatives.

On the one hand, he pointed out that nothing could be more economically catastrophic than a decline in consumer demand. Should buying lag, economic depression, or at least recession, becomes inevitable. Accordingly, consumers are "daily confronted with a barrage of advertising calculated to frighten or flatter them out of reasonable contentment into the nagging itch for goods and services [they] don't really need" (Sayers 1969, 145).

On the other hand, new consumer cravings had to be discovered and created. Nothing could be more economically destructive than an outbreak of widespread contentment. Were a majority of North Americans to remain content with last year's shoes, hats, clothes, cars, furniture, electronic gadgets, breakfast cereals, detergents, perfumes, hairstyles, and houses, the "good life" would sputter to an end. "To bring into being wants that did not previously exist" became the great mission of advertising and salesmanship—a process compared by economist

Galbraith to a humanitarian who, while impressing upon would-be donors the urgent need for more hospital facilities, inadvertently overlooks the fact that the local physician is running down pedestrians to keep the hospital fully occupied! As Galbraith laconically comments, "Among the many models of the good society, no one has urged the squirrel wheel" (Galbraith 1958, 124–28). In North America we have come close.

President George Bush's urgent appeal to Americans to go out and buy things as a patriotic response to 9/11 was both appropriate and predictable. The slump in consumer confidence, in response to the American subprime mortgage fiasco and subsequent Wall Street crash, brought America to its economic knees. Economists and politicians continue to wait hopefully for the day when large numbers of American consumers will once again rise to the occasion by living beyond their means, stretching the thin facade of prosperity over the dangerously fragile superstructure of personal indebtedness (McTevia 2010). Only this will redound to the glory of the financial and political plutocracy that has long ruled in the United States.

Theoretically, of course, American Christians do not countenance such a reductionist view of life. Yet, like frogs swimming in a gradually heating kettle of water, we find ourselves caught (or should I say, cooked!) in a way of life that our own Scriptures refer to as "idolatry" (Col 3:5) (Rosner 2007). Greed—the insistence on more than enough in the full awareness of many who have less than enough—is idolatry. Not surprisingly, American missionaries have not been immune to this elemental tendency in their society. True creatures of our times, no sooner does a new product appear than we missionaries discover a plausible reason for putting it into missionary service. Specialized suppliers exist whose "mission" is to ensure that Western missionaries do not become "out of date" in either their personal or missiological effects. Missionaries of today can congratulate themselves that the adjective "missionary"—when applied to wardrobe and equipment—no longer denotes the frumpy obsolescence it once did.

The culture in which most North American missionaries are born and bred has instilled within them the "need" for far more than their nineteenth and twentieth century counterparts dreamed possible. Nurtured in and supported by churches which, for the most part, have long since succumbed to the "spirit of the age" that engulfs them, the Western missionary enterprise has not been markedly resistant to the "Laodicean" phenomenon at either personal or institutional levels. Perhaps too much criticism of the status quo would cost prophetic missionaries the financial support of a wealthy and self-satisfied church; or, more likely, the frog has been in the kettle so long that it can no longer get out, even though the water temperature is now dangerously high.

We are now haunted by distressing indications that, for most of our fellow human beings, there neither is nor can be any possible road to our way of life, with its visions of ever-increasing levels of comfort and consumption. But since the only economic gospel that we Westerners can proclaim is the one that we personally model, we can do little more than keep running on our consumer treadmills. Quite apart from the factors alluded to above, the stark and brutal truth is that the natural resources of our planet are sufficient to support "developed" life for only a tiny fraction of its human population. Accordingly, emissaries of the Western churches must be prepared as never before to test the truthfulness of their assertion that "Christ is the answer" in the context of personal material want. At the very least, a missionary's personal stake in the most affluent and powerful civilization in the history of our planet needs to be acknowledged and considered when formulating a strategy for Christian mission of any kind.

But let me return to the subject of this paper. Christians—including those of us from affluent societies—will always be a pilgrim people, strangers in the land, bound for a city whose ruler and maker is God. Which missionary among us had anything directly to do with either our nation's ascendancy or its defining policies? In the colorful words of the once editor of the *Edinburgh Review*, we feel "like flies on the chariot wheel; perched upon a question of which we can neither see the diameter, nor control the motion, nor influence the moving force" (Russell 1905, 107) While the siren allure of manifest destiny in all of its self-congratulating and self-serving permutations is the natural fuel of the idolatry known as nationalism, even the most patriotic Christian, when confronted with the gulf between God's kingdom standards and his or her nation's self-serving agenda, admits to the impossibility of spanning the chasm. The truth is that no nation will ever be Christ-like. No nation will lay down its life for its enemies. No nation will love those who wish it ill, in the self-sacrificing spirit of our Lord. Nations are by definition self-serving and self-promoting, rather than Christ-serving and self-denying. The best a nation might manage is some form of Christendom. Whatever the accident of their national identities, Christ's followers are called to a better way. The gospel, after all, is not merely a prisoner of culture; it is the liberator of men and women held in thrall to God-defying impulses and institutions in their culture (Boyd 2004, 2005; Hughes 2009).

## Strategic Implications of Missionary Affluence

The relative affluence of missionaries, whether or not they are Western, has serious strategic implications of course, both positive and negative. Western mission strategies, beginning with the support of missionary personnel, are money intensive. Without ample supplies of money, missionary efforts from the West would be severely truncated. Indeed, it is safe to conjecture, they would virtually cease. American Protestant mission agencies reported a total income for overseas missions of $5.7 billion for 2008 (Weber 2010, 166). Distributed among eight hundred US agencies, 47,261 US personnel served overseas for more than one year with some 118,659 short-term "missionaries" serving from two weeks to less than a year. Canadian agencies reported a total 2008 income of $716.5 million supporting the work of 2,890 Canadian personnel serving overseas for more than one year and some 6,817 short-term missionaries serving an average of two weeks (Moreau 2011). The money of these efforts was used to finance a wide range of useful operations whose implementation and sustenance require the kind of financial and technological support available only in the West. Schools, books, hospitals, autoclaves, X-ray machines, vehicles, radio and television sending and receiving equipment, tractors, grain, airplanes, cars, jeeps, trucks, well-drilling machines, computers, scholarships, international conferences and consultations, and the myriad of other vital accoutrements of those mission strategies originating in the West require a scale of affluence unavailable anywhere else in the world. But above all, support of missionaries and their families was used to sustain a culturally defined level of personal entitlement.

## Relational Implications of Missionary Affluence

Possession of wealth virtually ensures missionary insulation. A primary advantage of wealth lies in its capacity to acquire goods and services that can cushion the wealthy from the harsh realities of life. All human beings desire not only to survive, but to proceed through life as comfortably as possible. Compared to the poor, we who are rich enjoy astounding comfort on our journey through life.

The word "insulate" is thought to have derived from the Latin *insulatus*— meaning "to make into an island." In its contemporary usage, the verb "to insulate" means "to prevent or reduce the transmission of electricity, heat, or sound to or from (a body, device, or region) by surrounding with a non-conducting material" (*Collins English Dictionary of the English Language* 1979, 758).

Both the etymology and the definition of this word are instructive in the context of the present discussion, since to a remarkable degree Western missionaries, because of their affluence, inhabit an island in a sea of poverty. Their affluence constitutes quite literally the "nonconducting material" which protects them from the "heat" and "sound" of the poverty in which the majority of the globe's inhabitants live and move and have their being. Since biblical faith is above all a relational faith, it is not only sad, but sinful, when personal possessions and privileges prevent, distort, or destroy the relationships of Christ's followers with the poor. But this appears to be an almost inevitable consequence of personal affluence.

Profoundly asymmetric socioeconomic statuses make genuine friendship extremely unlikely. Not only is it difficult for a rich person to enter the kingdom of heaven; it is almost impossible for them to establish deep friendships with poor people.

A friend is an intimate—someone with whom one generally has much in common. In their friendships, people naturally gravitate to those with whom they are not only temperamentally but socially and economically compatible. It is humanly almost impossible for a wealthy family to share a deeply fraternal relationship with a family whose material and economic resources are a pathetic fraction of their own; who cannot afford an education for their beloved children beyond minimal literacy, while the children of the wealthy family anticipate as a matter of course opportunity and money for education up to the very highest levels; whose house is a tiny one-room shack (made of straw or cardboard) with no amenities, while the wealthy family resides in a Western-style bungalow, complete with kitchen, bathroom, private bedrooms for each member of the family, carpeted floors, stuffed furniture, closets and bureaus filled with clothes, and personal servants; who must rely solely upon leg power to get anywhere, while the wealthy family has access to car, jeep, powerboat, or airplane; for whom the concept of vacation doesn't even exist, while the wealthy family spends one month of each year traveling and sightseeing, or simply taking it easy in a resort far away from the grind of everyday work.

Between families of widely disparate means and standards of living, friendship is extremely unlikely. With whom does a missionary naturally choose to spend leisure time? With whom is a vacation comfortably shared? Who is likely to listen comprehendingly, sympathetically, understandingly, to a couple as they pour out the peculiar frustrations, burdens, and perplexities of missionary parenting? With whom is a Western missionary likely to go shopping for family birthday or Christmas gifts? Who is able to commiserate with the missionary on the inadequacy of his or her support level? From whom will a missionary likely seek advice on personal financial matters—investment, banking, saving? In every case, it is very doubtful whether the poor would have any part in these aspects of a missionary's life. The social rapport required must obviously be reserved for social and economic peers. The presence of the poor in such situations would be an embarrassment to any missionary of even moderate sensitivity.

The staggeringly high relational price exacted for missionary affluence is compounded by wealth's insidious effects upon the communication process. Both the medium and the message are significantly affected by the dynamics of the interpersonal relationships necessarily entailed. Were the message of the cross merely a series of theologically correct propositions about God, fallen humanity, and eternal salvation, the obligation to preach the gospel could be fulfilled by means of remote public announcements, delivered by loudspeaker, radio, and television. But the Word must always be made flesh and dwell among men. And the Way has always best been shown by those who can be accompanied by would-be pilgrims. A missionary is above all a Way-shower, whose life can be imitated by his or her converts. The missionary is not simply a voice box, but a pilgrim who invites others to join him or her on the narrow way.

It is clear from the Bible that while we humans are social, communicating, and thinking creatures, we are—at root—profoundly theological beings, created in the image of God and inhabiting his moral universe. As such, there is no facet of a missionary's life or thought that does not in some way both reflect and affect his or her theology. While much more could be said about the strategic and relational implications of communicating the gospel from a vantage point of wealth and power, I move on to consideration of some profoundly ethical implications that emerge as a direct and inevitable consequence of relative missionary affluence.

## Theological Implications of Wealth

When within a given social context we are rich, it follows that what the Bible says to and about the rich, it says to and about us. Missionaries are not an exception to this rule. Wealth and poverty are among the most frequently recurring themes in our Christian Scriptures. While gross material inequity in close social proximity poses profound relational, communicatory, and strategic challenges for missionaries, as outlined above, more fundamental are the complex questions of ethical integrity that challenge any wealthy follower of Jesus moving in contexts of profound poverty. Among those of us who make our living by speaking for God and about

God, Christian missionaries—perhaps more than any other professional religious group—are acutely aware of the need for consistency between what we say we believe and how we actually live.

## POSSESSIONS, THE POOR, AND GOD'S PEOPLE

In both the Old and the New Testaments, there is a modest stream of teaching that reassures the rich: the sanctity of private property, the association of wealth with happiness, prosperity as a reward for righteousness, and the relationship between personal patterns of behavior and poverty. Such teaching is of no small comfort to those of us who, by whatever means, find ourselves in the happy state of relative comfort and affluence. We are permitted a measure of modest self-congratulation, together with opportunity to give thanks to God, the true source of our personal good fortune.

But any soothing theological reverie into which the materially blessed might sink is more than anticipated by the less flattering and painfully didactic portrayal of the rich that pervades both the Old and the New Testaments. This teaching, woven into the warp and woof of God's directives about what is good and appropriate for his people, is calculated to make those of us who are rich much less sanguine about our good fortune (Sider 1998, 10–12; Wallis 2000, 6–7).

I recall the story told to me by a missionary linguist working with Africa Inter-Mennonite Mission, Paul Thiessen, who, with his wife and children, lived and worked for several decades among the Siamou in Burkina Faso. As one of eight children born to a poor cobbler in a small Mennonite community in southern Manitoba, he recalled the shame of having to go to school wearing worn, hand-me-down clothes and shoes, and carrying a lunch of simple lard and bread sandwiches. A shy, naturally quiet boy, among some of his better memories was listening to his minister preaching on biblical themes that stressed God's concern for the poor and the prospect of frightful judgment for the rich.

As missionaries, he and his family settled in the largest village of Siamou-speaking people—a community of an estimated eight hundred. The most powerful man in the region was the chief, whose prestige was enhanced by his possession of an old, broken bicycle. As Paul began the work of Bible translation, the numerous passages from which he had once derived consolation now made him uncomfortable; the tables had been turned. Caught in the glare of God's word as interpreted by his neighbors, the status he now occupied left him and his family embarrassingly exposed, raising deep questions about their integrity. Here are some of the reasons why.

## Rights of Personal Wealth Subordinated to Obligation for the Poor

Divinely sanctioned guidelines were to be followed literally, and were intended to prevent a fragmentation of society into those who enjoyed perpetual economic advantage over those who suffered perpetual economic hardship. Included in the Mosaic guidelines were provisions for:

1. Recurring years of jubilee, when all land was to revert to its original owners—Leviticus 25:8–28;

2. A regular sabbatical year when debts were to be forgiven—Deuteronomy 15:1–6; 2 Chronicles 36:15–21;

3. Tithing every year, with the poor as primary beneficiaries every third year—Deuteronomy 14:22–29;

4. Strict guidelines, favoring the borrower, on loans, interest, and loan collateral—Leviticus 25:35–38; Deuteronomy 23:19,20; 24:6,10–13,17,18;

5. Gleaning regulations strictly for the benefit of the poor—Deuteronomy 24:19,20;

6. Debt repayment guidelines, favoring the poor—Deuteronomy 15:1–11;

7. Stipulations regarding treatment of employees by employers, favoring employees—Deuteronomy 24:14,15; and

8. Strict limitations on the wealth of kings—Deuteronomy 17:14–17; (cf. 1 Kgs 6–7; 11:1–6). The divine intention is clear: not only were the poor to be protected from exploitation; the law was designed to ensure that they were its chief beneficiaries.

## The Inherent Dangers of Wealth

Wealth is inherently dangerous and is frequently associated with fatally destructive personal and national orientations.

1. The prosperous tend to marginalize God—Deuteronomy 8:10–20.

2. Wealth is the natural culture in which pride and a self-deluding sense of security and self-congratulations (for a self-made man or nation) seem inevitably to flourish at both personal and national levels—Jeremiah 6:13–15; 12:1–4; 17:11; Ezekiel 28:4,5; 1 Timothy 6:6–19.

3. Wealth is almost inevitably associated with overindulgence, gluttony, and greed, which is idolatry—1 Kings 6–7; 10:14–29; 11:1–6; 1 Corinthians 5:9–11; Colossians 3:5. (Greed is the insistence on more than enough in contexts where your neighbors have less than enough.)

4. The wealthy frequently abuse personal power by mistreatment of the weak and contempt for the poor—1 Kings 10:14–29; cf. 1 Kings 12:1–24; Job 12:5; Jeremiah 22:13–17; Ezekiel 16:49; 22:25–29.

5. The priorities and orientations of the rich seem almost inevitably to be fatally misguided—Isaiah 5:7,8,20–23.

6. Personal overindulgence and craven respect for the wealthy compromise the integrity of those who claim to speak for God—Jeremiah 6:13–15; 8:10,11; Micah 2:6–11; 3:5,10,11.

7. Religious leaders and missionaries in the early days of the church who "loved money" warranted especially harsh criticism—Matthew 23:23–26; Luke 11:39–42; cf. Matthew 7:21–27; Luke 6:46; 11:28; 2 Corinthians 2:17.

8. Christ pronounced woes on the rich and made it clear that it was almost impossible for a rich man to inherit eternal life, and that to be a "wealthy disciple" comes close to being an oxymoron—Matthew 19:16–24; James 5:1–6.

9. Preoccupation with self, money, and pleasure are signs of a doomed, "last days" way of life—2 Timothy 3:1-5.

10. Personal wealth demands absorption in mammon, deadening a person's or a nation's sense of their spiritual destitution—Matthew 13:22; 22:5; Luke 12:13-21; Revelation 3:14-21. (The Laodicean church, apparently surfeited with mammon, lacked the most elementary Christian essential, Christ himself!)

11. Wealth never satisfies, but breeds covetousness and greed, a continual desire for more—Ephesians 4:17-19; 5:3-11. Our Lord's description of those whose hearts are weighed down with "dissipation"—unrestrained indulgence in the pursuit of pleasure—is an apt description of consumers and consumerism (Luke 21:34-36). Such teaching should give sober pause to Christians living as aliens and strangers in a culture in which the pursuit of happiness is a constitutionally guaranteed right of every citizen. When this orientation to life is on conspicuous display in contexts of poverty, certain consequences are inevitable (Packer 2002).

## The Association of Wealth with Unrighteousness

Wealth and prosperity are often signs of greed-driven exploitation of the poor—Job 21:7-16; Proverbs 13:23; Isaiah 32:7.

1. Faithfulness to God is no guarantee of personal prosperity or security—Jeremiah 44:15-18.

2. Not only is it possible to have too little, it is possible to have too much—Proverbs 30:8,9.

3. Not just active oppression, but complacent neglect of the poor leads inexorably to judgment—Deuteronomy 8:19,20; 28:15; 2 Chronicles 36:15-21.

4. Religious orthodoxy without practical concern for the poor is a hollow sham—Isaiah 1:10-23.

## God Identifies with the Poor

Laws given in Exodus 22:21–27 demonstrate God's concern for the poor and the oppressed. This identification was demonstrated in several ways.

1. God came as one of them—Psalm 22; Isaiah 53. Jesus was born in a stable and, judging from the nature of their temple offering at his dedication, his parents were far from rich—Luke 1:46–56; 2:1–20,21–24; cf. Leviticus 12:8. Jesus' first recorded public words related to the poor—Matthew 15:31–46; Luke 4:18–30.

2. God's children are marked by their proactive concern for the poor and the oppressed—Job 30:24,25; 31:16–28; Amos 5:4–24; 6:4–7; 8:4–7.

3. God meets the needs of the poor through the actions and interventions of his obedient people. This was the intent of the laws dealing with the treatment of the poor by the rich—Nehemiah 5:1–13.

4. Christ's true followers proactively identify with the poor in practical, costly ways—Matthew 23:1–39; 25:31–46.

## Economic Repentance Is Both Costly and Rare

The powerful and wealthy customarily deal with prophetic preaching by dismissing or destroying the preacher and engaging the services of those willing to offer a more sanguine interpretation of their inflated sense of personal entitlement and relative self-indulgence—Isaiah 30:9–11. A rare Old Testament account of repentance is found in Nehemiah 5:1–12, while in the New Testament Zacchaeus serves as a rare example in Luke 19:1–9. In the early days of the church, rich Christians were commanded "not to be arrogant nor to put their hope in wealth … to do good, to be rich in good deeds, and to be generous and willing to share" (1Tim 6:17–19). Repentance without the fruit of repentance is meaningless—Micah 6:6–16.

## DISPARITY: RECOGNITION AND RESPONSE

For those of us who are wealthy in a land where most people enjoy an abundance of possessions, and where the poor are kept out of sight in ghettos and on reservations, biblical teaching on wealth and poverty is vaguely disquieting. Of course, we are well aware that our planet is home to vast numbers of impoverished and even destitute peoples, and that some of them live not far away. But any niggling disquiet of conscience that we might feel—usually sparked by fleetingly surreal images on our flat-screen television sets—is easily quelled. What, after all, do such people have to do with us? Our very helplessness in the face of endemic human tragedy is, in its own way, mercifully reassuring. But when the spiritual leader of a congregation is the one person enjoying a relatively lavish standard of living, biblical teaching becomes more difficult to either explain or model. It is this that is most problematic for a wealthy missionary.

This, then, is the substance of my argument, here reiterated:

1. Western missionaries frequently discover themselves to be relatively wealthy within their ministry contexts.

2. When this is so, what the Bible says to and about the wealthy, it says to and about the missionaries themselves.

3. Since the Christian faith is above all a relational faith, lived out in actual social and cultural contexts, the whole gospel is potentially contradicted, obscured, or subverted by the good news of plenty, of which the missionary himself or herself constitutes "exhibit A."

4. In addition to the multifaceted communicatory, strategic, and relational consequences issuing from a missionary's relative affluence, fundamental ethical questions must be addressed because of scriptural teaching on the relationship between rich and poor, and between God's people and their possessions.

Conscientious missionaries have tended to respond to this state of affairs in one of four ways:

1. They might associate primarily with those of approximately equal social and economic privilege, and carry out ministry among the poor on a strictly "personage-to-personage" basis;

2. They might assume a simple lifestyle that they hope belies the extent of their privilege, while surreptitiously maintaining the benefits of Western entitlement in critical areas such as medical care, transportation, education of children, and retirement;

3. They might shift the debate from the moral/ethical dimensions of gross economic inequity among Christians living in close social proximity, on the one hand, to the realm of mission strategy and the merits of church independence vis-à-vis interdependence; and finally,

4. They might adopt a radically incarnational lifestyle, giving up privilege and living as those among whom they minister.

While each of these approaches can be defended on practical grounds, I am proposing a fifth approach: the appropriation of a biblically informed and contextually appropriate status of "righteous rich."

## A MISSIOLOGY OF THE "RIGHTEOUS RICH"?

When I wrote the first edition of my book on *Missions and Money*, my concluding chapter—bravely titled "Grappling with Affluence"—made vague calls to bring missionary lifestyles and strategies into conformity with New Testament teaching on the incarnation, as both theologically descriptive and strategically prescriptive; with the cross—as both symbol of the atonement and prescription for the only way of life promised to the followers of Jesus; and weakness—as channel of God's transforming power. But I was unable to specify just what this change might entail. I invited readers to become part of an ill-defined, inchoate "Fellowship of Venturers in Simpler Living" (Bonk 1991, 111–32), and to this day receive a trickle of letters from idealistic, conscience-stricken Western missionaries wrestling with complex personal questions regarding lifestyle, sharing, tithing, children's education, health care, and retirement.

If the second edition of my book is more constructive in its conclusions, this is due in large part to the contributions of Christopher J. H. Wright, who wrote a chapter entitled "The Righteous Rich in the Old Testament" (Bonk 2006, 191–201) and to Justo L. Gonzalez, who wrote two chapters: "New Testament Koinonía and Wealth" and "Wealth in the Subapostolic Church" (ibid., 203–21, 223–25). To the extent that my thinking on these matters has moved toward a more helpfully constructive conclusion—and I cannot be the judge of that—I am indebted to both the writings and the example of Jacob A. Loewen (1922–2008) and his wife, Anne, venerable Christian pilgrims, missionaries, linguists, and anthropologists (Loewen 1967; Loewen 1975, 412–43).

Each individual in any society is defined by a series of statuses, acknowledged and recognized by other members of that society. It is understood that each status carries with it certain roles and their associated behavioral expectations, which vary with the social context. Human identities and relationships are shaped by the complex interplay of recognized statuses, roles, and self-images that comprise the society. In the words of Loewen:

> Roles are the traditional ways people act in given situations. They are learned within the cultural setting. Very frequently the missionary is quite unconscious of this inventory of roles which he brings with him, and so never questions their legitimacy. But we must point out that even the very role of a missionary—a person paid by a foreign source to live in a strange country and to preach a new religion—is quite difficult for most people to understand. (1967, 291)

For a missionary's communication of the gospel to be effective, teaching must be accompanied by personal behavioral and character traits that are consistent with what is being taught. Role sincerity is absolutely crucial to missionary integrity. Those who make a living by being religious are often tempted to act and speak as if all the points they make are personal convictions. When this happens, role insincerity functions as a contradicting paramessage. As the old adage notes, "What you are speaks so loud that the world can't hear what you say."

Loewen points out that until a newcomer has been duly incorporated into the established network of relationships, members of a society will not know how to act toward him or her. This is why early explorers and traders in North America often found it necessary to become blood brothers to individual tribesmen. Once such a link had been established, the whole group knew how to behave toward the newcomer, even though the newcomer might not yet know what was expected of him. While most societies allow for a period of trial and error for newcomers to learn to play their roles appropriately, if a newcomer persists in unpredictable or inappropriate behavior beyond the allowed limit, he or she will be judged to be unreliable at best, perhaps even false.

A related problem arises from "roles" appropriated by a new missionary. He or she behaves in ways which, in that society—unbeknownst to the missionary— mark him or her as belonging to a given status. When the missionary fulfills only a part of expected behavior associated with the status and its accompanying roles, there are problems, and people can feel deeply betrayed or angry. For example, many missionaries, in an effort to help people economically, have unwittingly assumed the role of patron or feudal master. When they then refuse to fulfill the obligations associated with that role, people are confused, frustrated, and even angry. They question the sincerity and honesty of that missionary (Loewen 1975, 426–27).

I would like to propose that Christians generally, including missionaries— whenever they either anticipate or discover that their way of life and its entitlements make them rich by the standards of those around them—embrace the status of "righteous rich" and learn to play its associated roles in ways that are both culturally appropriate and biblically informed.

It is clear that the Christian Scriptures draw a sharp distinction between the righteous who are prosperous and the rich who are unrighteous, and that the distinction between the two is determined chiefly on the basis of their respective dealings with the poor. It would seem absolutely vital for missionaries to make the biblical study of this subject an essential part of both their preparation and their ongoing spiritual journey.

Representative of this genre of scriptural teaching are five texts—three from the Old Testament and two from the New Testament:

## Job 29:11–17

Whoever heard me spoke well of me, and those who saw me commended me, because I rescued the poor who cried for help, and the fatherless who had none to assist them. The man who was dying blessed me; I made the widow's heart sing. I put on righteousness as my clothing; justice was my robe and my turban. I was eyes to the blind and feet to the lame. I was a father to the needy; I took up the case of the stranger. I broke the fangs of the wicked and snatched the victims from their teeth.

## Job 31:16–28

If I have denied the desires of the poor or let the eyes of the widow grow weary, if I have kept my bread to myself, not sharing it with the fatherless—but from my youth I reared them as a father would, and from my birth I guided the widow—if I have seen anyone perishing for lack of clothing, or the needy without garments, and their hearts did not bless me for warming them with the fleece from my sheep, if I have raised my hand against the fatherless, knowing that I had influence in court, then let my arm fall from the shoulder, let it be broken off at the joint. For I dreaded destruction from God, and for fear of his splendor I could not do such things.

If I have put my trust in gold or said to pure gold, "You are my security," if I have rejoiced over my great wealth, the fortune my hands had gained, if I have regarded the sun in its radiance or the moon moving in splendor, so that my heart was secretly enticed and my hand offered them a kiss of homage, then these also would be sins to be judged, for I would have been unfaithful to God on high.

Whether we subscribe to the "hidden hand of the market" as the source of all good things, or whether we detect in the regional, national, and global marketplace the not-so-hidden hand of the economically and politically powerful, it is clear that Job understood himself to be personally responsible for playing a proactive role in the material well-being of poor people in his orbit, and that this is the way God wanted him to be. At the very least, a wealthy missionary will need to be prepared to explain why God-fearing Western missionaries should be considered exempt from this ancient standard, and whether God has changed his mind since Adam Smith in the eighteenth century so kindly rectified the muddled idealism of apparently unworkable Mosaic economics.

## Deuteronomy 15:1–11

At the end of every seven years you must cancel debts. This is how it is to be done: Every creditor shall cancel any loan they have made to a fellow Israelite. They shall not require payment from anyone among their own people, because the LORD's time for canceling debts has been proclaimed. You may require payment from a foreigner, but you must cancel any debt your fellow Israelite owes you. However, there need be no poor people among you, for in the land the LORD your God is giving you to possess as your inheritance, he will richly bless you, if only you fully obey the LORD your God and are careful to follow all these commands I am giving you today. For the LORD your God will bless you as he has promised, and you will lend to many nations but will borrow from none. You will rule over many nations but none will rule over you.

If anyone is poor among your fellow Israelites in any of the towns of the land the LORD your God is giving you, do not be hardhearted or tightfisted toward them. Rather, be openhanded and freely lend them whatever they need. Be careful not to harbor this wicked thought: "The seventh year, the year for canceling debts, is near," so that you do not show ill will toward the needy among your fellow Israelites and give them nothing. They may then appeal to the LORD against you, and you will be found guilty of sin. Give generously to them and do so without a grudging heart; then because of this the LORD your God will bless you in all your work and in everything you put your hand to. There will always be poor people in the land. Therefore I command you to be openhanded toward your fellow Israelites who are poor and needy in your land.

If the principles, ideals, and objectives outlined in the Deuteronomy 15:1–11 (cf. Lev 25:8–17) passage have any kind of legitimacy across time and cultures, one may well ask whether any nations today could be deemed righteous. Whether or not such practical concerns should be expected to characterize Western nations—descended from a Christendom that was and is far from Christian—the people of God, especially missionaries, must explain how the relationship between rich and poor is to be addressed in similarly appropriate and practical ways today.

## Nehemiah 5:1–12

Now the men and their wives raised a great outcry against their fellow Jews. Some were saying, "We and our sons and daughters are numerous; in order for us to eat and stay alive, we must get grain."

Others were saying, "We are mortgaging our fields, our vineyards and our homes to get grain during the famine."

Still others were saying, "We have had to borrow money to pay the king's tax on our fields and vineyards. Although we are of the same flesh and blood as our fellow Jews and though our children are as good as theirs, yet we have to subject our sons and daughters to slavery. Some of our daughters have already been enslaved, but we are powerless, because our fields and our vineyards belong to others."

When I heard their outcry and these charges, I was very angry. I pondered them in my mind and then accused the nobles and officials. I told them, "You are charging your own people interest!" So I called together a large meeting to deal with them and said: "As far as possible, we have bought back our fellow Jews who were sold to the Gentiles. Now you are selling your own people, only for them to be sold back to us!" They kept quiet, because they could find nothing to say.

So I continued, "What you are doing is not right. Shouldn't you walk in the fear of our God to avoid the reproach of our Gentile enemies? I and my brothers and my men are also lending the people money and grain. But let us stop charging interest! Give back to them immediately their fields, vineyards, olive groves and houses, and also the interest you are charging them—one percent of the money, grain, new wine and olive oil."

"We will give it back," they said. "And we will not demand anything more from them. We will do as you say."

Then I summoned the priests and made the nobles and officials take an oath to do what they had promised.

For those of us who are wealthy, it is sobering to find in the Scriptures scarcely any record of repentance on the part of the rich. Here in Nehemiah is one heartening instance, a reminder that no matter how complicated the issues or how deeply entrenched and personally vested the self-interests, it is possible to repent. What would repentance look like from the vantage point of powerful mission organizations in contexts of poverty? That is difficult to say, since the righteous rich missionary or mission agency, while informed biblically, must be defined contextually.

## 1 John 3:16–20

This is how we know what love is: Jesus Christ laid down his life for us. And we ought to lay down our lives for our brothers and sisters. If anyone has material possessions and sees a brother or sister in need but has no pity on them, how can the love of God be in that person? Dear children, let us not love with words or speech but with actions and in truth.

This is how we know that we belong to the truth and how we set our hearts at rest in his presence: If our hearts condemn us, we know that God is greater than our hearts, and he knows everything.

This passage, and many others like it, makes acutely uncomfortable public reading when wealthy missionaries serve in contexts of dire poverty.

## 1 Timothy 6:6–10, 17–19

But godliness with contentment is great gain. For we brought nothing into the world, and we can take nothing out of it. But if we have food and clothing, we will be content with that. Those who want to get rich fall into temptation and a trap and into many foolish and harmful desires that plunge people into ruin and destruction. For the love of money is a root of all kinds of evil. Some people, eager for money, have wandered from the faith and pierced themselves with many griefs …

Command those who are rich in this present world not to be arrogant nor to put their hope in wealth, which is so uncertain, but to put their hope in God, who richly provides us with everything for our enjoyment. Command them to do good, to be rich in good deeds, and to be generous and willing to share. In this way they will lay up treasure for themselves as a firm foundation for the coming age, so that they may take hold of the life that is truly life.

Contained in these texts are the minimal guidelines—"righteous rich templates" in a manner of speaking—that should guide the righteous rich, whatever their time or place. That such standards will be applied to wealthy missionaries by the poor among whom they live and work is a certainty. And so they should be. The challenge for any wealthy missionary will be to make sure that he or she is seen as righteous, according to the standards of the group in which he or she lives and works, and above all, in ways that consistently reflect the mind of Christ whom he or she represents.

I have been involved in the training and nurturing of missionaries for much of my adult life. For the past eight years, I have had the extraordinary privilege of serving Christian leaders and missionaries from around the world at the Overseas Ministries Study Center in New Haven, Connecticut, USA, through our community and programs assisting them in their quest for spiritual, professional, and intellectual renewal. It is natural, then, that I should bring my chapter to a conclusion by proposing that our training and retraining curricula and on-field orientations should include courses and forums for serious, sustained discussion of this troublesome issue. To my knowledge, systematic exploration of the dynamics and missiological implications of economic inequity in close social proximity is not usually a part of missionary training, on-field orientation, or postgraduate mission studies. Included in every mission studies curriculum should be at least one seminar exploring biblical teaching on wealth and poverty, the rich and the poor, with implications drawn and applications made for Christian missions and missionaries.

## GOD'S MISSION IN GOD'S WORLD IN GOD'S WAY

Throughout the William Carey Era, the Western missionary enterprise has been marked by prodigious and impressive efforts to account for all the peoples of the world—locating, registering, and classifying them in its missiological ledgers (Carey 1792; Barrett 1982). Late in 2001, the long-awaited *World Christian Trends AD 30–AD 2200: Interpreting the Annual Christian Megacensus* made its debut (Barrett and Johnson 2001). Without doubt one of the most extraordinary reference works to be published in the last decade, this impressive supplement to the second edition of the *World Christian Encyclopedia* is comprised of 934 pages of statistics, analyses, speculation, and maps. Included is a fifty-nine-page overview of "1,500 global plans to evangelize the world" (ibid., 779–838). In addition to much useful information, the authors have indulged in some highly imaginative futurism in the "Cosmochronology" section of the volume (ibid., 93–209).

Concepts in keeping with such broad-brush thinking have been a mainstay of Western missiology, and have included such ambitious enterprises as the "DAWN 2000" strategy (Montgomery 1989, vii), the "AD 2000 and Beyond Movement" (Bush 1992), and the "Adopt-A-People Clearinghouse" (ibid.), with an appropriate lexicon replete with such terms as "10/40 Window" or "unreached peoples" (Bush 2003). Some ten years before the publication of their magnum opus, as one volume of the impressive "AD 2000 series," Barrett and Johnson oversaw production of a 136-page volume, "the brainchild of a team of twenty-six missiologists and researchers comprising the Global Statistics Task Force" by graphic means of diagrams, charts, and statistics laying out "the hard data [needed to set mission strategies] for the nineties" (Barrett and Johnson 1990, iii and back cover).

Such studies represent the modus operandi of the powerful Western church, and they complement global church growth figures that are astounding. According to figures appearing in the January 2010 issue of the *International Bulletin of Missionary Research*, between 1900 and 2010 the number of self-confessed Christians increased from 558,131,000 to 2,292,454,000. Of these, "Great Commission Christians" (defined as "active church members of all traditions who take Christ's Great Commission seriously") increased from 77,918,000 to 706,806,000 (Johnson et al. 2010, 36).

As impressive as such studies and figures are, however, and despite the prodigious efforts of tens of thousands of Christian missionaries over the past two centuries, the expansion of the church is not even keeping pace with population growth. Whereas in 1900 Christians represented 34.5 percent of the total population, by 2010 their proportion had slipped to 33.2 percent. While global annual population growth is projected at 1.23 percent, annual growth trends for Christianity are projected to be a paltry 0.08 percent. More encouragingly, Pentecostal/charismatic numbers are growing at 2.24 percent, while "Great Commission Christian" numbers are increasing at 1.14 percent (ibid.). Not only is there much work to be done, but the effective work that is being done is almost inevitably traceable to unsung incarnational and indigenous missionaries.

## Interruptions and God's Good News

Truly *Christian* mission is never ethereal or speculative. It is always incarnational, always parochial, and always addresses real human beings at the point of their personal circumstances, whatever the larger context, over which neither we nor they have any control. Effective mission can never be merely the byproduct of clever corporate strategizing and coolly calculated actions. It has always and will always be the natural activity of passionate believers who cannot help but speak those things they have seen and heard.

Allow me to reflect briefly on the central act of the cosmic drama in which Christian missions play a part: the birth, life, death, and resurrection of one who, against the backdrop of his contemporary Roman Empire movers and shakers two thousand years ago, seemed utterly insignificant.

Put yourself at the corporate board table where the Creator/Chairman announces that he wants to save a world that slipped out of his grasp when the crown of his creation, human beings, chose to alienate themselves from their Creator. The Creator/CEO so loves those whom he has created in his own image that he is not willing for any of them to perish. Those who bear his image, who are infused with his very DNA, are in desperate need of redemption, but they are scattered across five continents. Fortunately, the Creator/CEO has a few advantages: he is omnipresent, omniscient, and omnipotent! Communication will be no problem for the Omnipresent One; a workable strategy should be simplicity itself for the Omniscient One; and command of the methods and resources requisite to the task can hardly be insurmountable for the Omnipotent One.

So what does God do? Overriding all common sense and good advice, he sends his only begotten Son into the world as a child, born out of wedlock to a peasant mother and a carpenter stepfather, in an occupied back eddy of a relentlessly powerful and brutal empire. The details of his birth are not very clear. Except that he arrived not in the maternity ward of the best medical facility that the power of his day could provide, but in a stable, in the presence of an assortment of common barnyard animals.

These doubtful witnesses were joined in attesting to his birth by shepherds, so notoriously unreliable that their word was deemed legally unacceptable as testimony. The child was born outside the power and privilege structures of the day. No newsmen were present, and no cameras were on hand to capture on film the central act of the long drama of our moral universe. Later, Eastern seers—astrologers really, given to elaborately fantastic speculations about the future—not only acknowledged him as a promised king but unwittingly jeopardized his life, forcing his parents to become refugees before the child was two years old. These seers, one can say with some certainty, would not be given the time of day in most contemporary evangelical churches.

As he grew and developed, we are told that he had to learn obedience, just like any other child. We know almost nothing about his early years, except that his parents had to flee with him to Egypt to escape Herod. Once again, as in the highly inconvenient circumstances surrounding his birth, a powerful political entity, claiming the proprietary right to self-serving violence that is always the prerogative of the powerful, seemed to have the upper hand over the Son of God. What Jesus and his parents did when they finally returned to Nazareth we do not know. Joseph and Mary continued to have children—stepbrothers and stepsisters to whom Jesus was the eldest brother. Presumably Joseph and his sons worked as carpenters. They were devout, and no doubt attended the synagogue and made an annual trip to the temple in Jerusalem.

Aside from his seemingly thoughtless adolescent behavior when he remained in the temple debating and caused his frantic parents no end of worry concerning his whereabouts, we learn only that "Jesus grew in wisdom and stature, and in favor with God and man" (Luke 2:52). Other than this, of Jesus' formative years we know nothing.

Even for the last three eventful years of his life, Gospel accounts provide only fragmentary information on what he did and how he busied himself in accomplishing his Father's plans for the world. A careful reading of the four Gospels tells us mostly about pesky interruptions. With a mandate to save the world, Jesus seems to be constantly dragged into the petty but time-consuming, schedule-interrupting agendas of persons from the lowest strata of society: blind beggars, cripples, sick children, anxious parents, diseased lepers, the psychologically deranged, and so on. He was often attacked by devoutly orthodox, Bible-believing leaders of his time because of his radical, at times "blasphemous," reinterpretation of the sacred text. He was particularly tactless in his encounters with these very people whose goodwill he should have carefully cultivated. These God fearers are greatly relieved when, after immense and prolonged effort, they manage to get rid of this dangerous troublemaker, watching him die on a Roman cross between two thieves. "Thank God," they whisper. "If you are the Son of God, come down off the cross," they jeer, unaware that, had he done so, they and we would have been eternally doomed.

Today, of course, it is Jesus, rather than Caesar, who is remembered and who continues to wield influence. For us North American Christians whose material privilege and its concomitant power and prestige exceeds that of 90 percent of this planet's inhabitants, it is important to remember that God has not changed his ways and continues to prefer astoundingly anti-intuitive ways in accomplishing his purposes. Because we inhabit his moral universe, close association with brute power, vast organizations, skillful administrations, and large sums of money are not the key or even a key to God's eternal purposes for humankind.

## Willing to Be Useful in God's Way

A missiology of the righteous rich is, at its core, no more than a willingness to be useful in terms defined by the local contexts and people. For this there can be no better exemplar than our Lord himself. With a mission more sweeping in scope and magnitude than those of even the most daring mission strategists, his commission was to save the world. Oddly, by the standards of Western missions, he spent his life as a laughably parochial figure, rarely venturing in his actual ministry beyond the borders of his own foreign-occupied country. By the standards of even the most forgiving mission administrators, he proved to be frustratingly deficient when it came to actually fulfilling his mission. His major difficulty seemed to have been the interruptions that intruded into his larger plans for the world.

Almost everything written in the Gospel accounts of his life relates directly or indirectly to the wrenching, but strategically petty, personal agendas of the ordinary men and women who pressed in on him on all sides during the few short years of his ministry. The Creator God incarnate, bent on saving the whole world, allowed himself to be interrupted by the sick, the lame, the blind, the withered, the bereaved, the outcasts, the pariahs, the deaf, the demon possessed, the grieving. Whatever he may have been doing at the time, he seemed never too busy or tired to stop and pay close attention to their agendas.

How understandable it would have been for Jesus to regretfully turn away the ordinary people who constantly sought his attention, reminding them that as Creator of their planet, now charged with redeeming it, he simply did not have time to give attention to the personal details of their everyday lives. Instead, he demonstrated that any proclamation of the good news that does not intersect with the actual needs of ordinary people is not good news, but mere religious propaganda. On this issue he was at distinct odds with the Pharisees, as his followers today should be.

It is trite to remind ourselves that it was his willingness to yield to one final, fatal interruption on a hill just outside Jerusalem that accomplished our redemption. It is this interruption that lies at the heart of the gospel that takes missionaries to the ends of the earth. Defined and driven by corporate and ecclesiastical agendas that are the product of organizations and well-meaning church leaders often thousands of miles away, we sometimes have no time to serve people on their own terms, thereby implicitly denying both that we are servants at the beck and call of those among whom we minister, and that they, rather than we, ultimately determine our usefulness.

We missionaries who hail from some of the world's most affluent societies—with our possessions, our positions, and our power—have a lot to learn from our Lord. But we can learn! Were the role of "righteous rich" to be widely appropriated by Western missionaries, it is safe to assume that this would revolutionize the missionary enterprise. We would at once become more Christ-like—not merely comfortably accoutred promulgators of admirably correct propositions about God and inherited notions of ecclesiology, but righteous rich followers of Jesus, with our immense good fortune at the disposal of the communities in which we live and move as servants of God.

Christian mission that is successful by God's standards will be undertaken by women and men possessed by God, aware that they are doing God's work in God's world, and that this work is to be done in God's way. God has always used "ordinary" individuals whose identification with Christ makes it impossible for them to remain silent or sit still within contexts over which neither they nor their listeners have any control. These men and women are among us today. They are gripped by what they have witnessed and therefore believe with all their hearts, and they cannot help but speak. And they are turning the world upside down.

## REFERENCES

Barrett, David B. 1982. *World Christian encyclopedia: A comparative study of churches and religions in the modern world, AD 1900–2000.* London: Oxford University Press.

Barrett, David B., and Todd M. Johnson. 1990. *Our globe and how to reach it: Seeing the world evangelized by AD 2000 and beyond.* Birmingham, AL: New Hope.

———. 2001. *World Christian trends AD 30–AD 2200: Interpreting the annual Christian megacensus.* Pasadena: William Carey Library.

Bellah, Robert N., Richard Madsen, William M. Sullivan, Ann Swidler, and Steven M. Tipton. 1985. *Habits of the heart: Individualism and commitment in American life.* Berkeley: University of California Press.

Bonk, Jonathan. 1989. Missions and mammon: Six theses. *International Bulletin of Missionary Research* 13, no. 3: 174–81.

———. 1991. *Missions and money.* Maryknoll, NY: Orbis Books.

———. 2006. *Missions and money: Affluence as a missionary problem—revisited.* Maryknoll, NY: Orbis Books.

Boyd, Gregory A. 2004. The Cross and the sword. Sermon series presented at Woodland Hills Church, St. Paul, Minnesota.

———. 2005. *The myth of a Christian nation: How the quest for political power is destroying the church.* Grand Rapids: Zondervan.

Bush, Luis, ed. 1992. *AD 2000 and beyond handbook: A church for every people and the gospel for every person by AD 2000.* Pasadena: William Carey Library.

———. 2003. The AD2000 movement as a Great Commission catalyst. In *Between past and future: Evangelical mission entering the twenty-first century,* ed. Jonathan J. Bonk, 17–36. Evangelical Missiological Society Series, no. 10. Pasadena: William Carey Library.

Carey, William. 1792. *An enquiry into the obligations of Christians to use means for the conversion of the heathens.* Leicester, UK: Ann Ireland.

*Collins English dictionary of the English language.* 1979. New York: HarperCollins.

De Neui, Paul. 2010. *Family and faith in Asia: The missional impact of social networks.* Pasadena: William Carey Library.

East, David Jonathon. 1844. *Western Africa: Its condition, and Christianity the means of its recovery.* London: Houlston & Stoneman.

Galbraith, John Kenneth. 1958. *The affluent society.* Boston: Houghton Mifflin.

Henry, Jules. 1963. *Culture against man.* New York: Random House.

Hughes, Richard T. 2009. *Christian America and the kingdom of God.* Chicago: University of Illinois Press.

Jansen, Frank Kaleb, ed. 1993. *A church for every people: A list of unreached and adoptable peoples.* Colorado Springs: Adopt-A-People Clearinghouse, copublished with AD 2000 and Beyond Movement, MARC, Southern Baptist Convention—Foreign Mission Board, SIL, and US Center for World Mission.

Johnson, Todd M., David B. Barrett, and Peter F. Crossing. 2010. Christianity 2010: A view from the new atlas of global Christianity. *International Bulletin of Missionary Research* 34, no. 1 (January): 29–36.

Loewen, Jacob A. 1967. Missions and the problems of cultural background. In *The church in mission: A sixtieth anniversary tribute to J. B. Toews,* ed. A. J. Klassen, 286–318. Fresno: Mennonite Brethren Church.

———. 1975. *Culture and human values: Christian intervention in anthropological perspective.* Pasadena: William Carey Library.

MacDonald, Allan John. 1916. *Trade, politics, and Christianity in Africa and the East.* London: Longmans, Green and Co.

McTevia, James V. 2010. *The culture of debt: How a once-proud society mortgaged its future.* Bingham Farms, MI: McTevia and Associates.

Montgomery, Jim. 1989. *DAWN 2000: 7 million churches to go; The personal story of the DAWN strategy for world evangelization.* Pasadena: William Carey Library.

Moreau, Scott. 2011. A current snapshot of North American Protestant missions. *International Bulletin of Missionary Research* 35, no. 1 (January): 12–16.

Packer, George. 2002. When here sees there. *NY Times Magazine,* April 21.

Rosner, Brian S. 2007. *Greed as idolatry: The origin and meaning of a Pauline metaphor.* Grand Rapids: Eerdmans.

Russell, W. E. 1905. *Sydney Smith.* London: MacMillan.

Sayers, Dorothy. 1969. *Letters to a post-Christian world: A selection of essays.* Grand Rapids: Eerdmans.

Shi, David E. 1985. *The simple life: Plain living and high thinking in American culture.* New York: Oxford University Press.

Shoemaker, H. Stephen. 2006. *Being Christian in an almost chosen nation: Thinking about faith and politics.* Nashville: Abingdon.

Sider, Ronald. 1998. Jesus must weep. *The Mennonite,* August 25.

Smith, Stephen C. 2005. *Ending global poverty: A guide to what works.* New York: Palgrave Macmillan.

Wallis, Jim. 2000. A Bible full of holes. *The Mennonite,* November 21.

Weber, Linda, ed. 2010. *Mission handbook: U.S. and Canadian Protestant ministries overseas.* Chicago: EMIS.

Whybrow, Peter C. 2005. *American mania: When more is not enough.* New York: Norton.

Zinbarg, Edward D. 2005. *Faith, morals, and money: What the world's religions tell us about ethics in the marketplace.* New York: Continuum International.

Prison Book Project
PO Box 592
Titusville, FL 32781

# 5

# PARTNERSHIPS, MONEY, AND DIALOGUE IN BUDDHIST CONTEXTS

## Mary T. Lederleitner

In an idyllic world Christian leaders from every nation would share similar expectations when partnering together in ministry. However, this is rarely the case. By the time we reach an age of maturity where we can begin partnering with people from other cultures, a myriad of influences have been at work shaping our expectations. For this reason, if Western missionaries hope to partner well in diverse Buddhist contexts, mission leaders need tools to better understand one another's expectations. Kurt Lewin, a renowned voice in business literature, said that "nothing is so practical as a good theory" (Isaacs 1999, 74). An understanding of the theory known as the Ecology of Human Development can be a tremendous tool for those trying to design and contextualize cross-cultural partnerships. When coupled with an understanding of what dialogue is, and what it looks like in a Buddhist context, church planters and mission leaders are able to form partnerships that will foster better relationships and outcomes. Since "the most common quarrels in partnership focus upon the control, use, and accountability of money" (Gupta and Lingenfelter 2006, 200), special attention will be given to how these two tools can help partners navigate such complexities (Lederleitner 2010b).

## DIVERSITY PRESENT IN BUDDHIST CONTEXTS

Research indicates that the countries with the highest populations of Buddhists are China, Japan, Thailand, Vietnam, Myanmar, Sri Lanka, Cambodia, India, South Korea and Taiwan (Compare Infobase Limited 2006). Buddhism is also practiced extensively in countries such as Laos, Brunei and Bhutan, as well as by smaller percentages of people in several other countries around the world. Is a fifty-year-old pastor born and raised in Myanmar going to have the same expectations when he enters a cross-cultural ministry partnership as will a twenty-eight-year-old youth pastor from a megachurch in Shanghai? Both leaders are likely to bring great strengths to a ministry partnership. The pastor in Myanmar might be a seasoned and deeply respected ministry leader in his country. Partnering with him might open greater doors for evangelism and church planting. The youth pastor from Shanghai might be especially adept and creative at using technology to reach young people in China.

Both pastors are living and working within Buddhist countries, and both might be especially strategic to have as partners. However, their expectations about practical issues within the partnership, such as how decisions will be made, how funding will be utilized, and how reporting will be handled, are likely to be quite different. Frequently ministry partners want a template outlining how to do partnership in a specific region in the world. However, there is no "one size fits all" approach for doing partnership well in Buddhist contexts. Even within the same country or city, ministry leaders can enter partnerships with very different expectations. Given the diversity and what it means to partner in a Buddhist context, broader systems of human development must be considered, as well as issues of faith, if we hope to unearth expectations held by cross-cultural ministry partners.

## WHAT IS THE ECOLOGY OF HUMAN DEVELOPMENT?

The Ecology of Human Development is a theory which proposes that human beings do not develop in a vacuum but rather are profoundly impacted and shaped by multiple levels of influence. Those influences are embedded in various systems, some of which people relate with personally and others of which they are wholly unaware. Rather than being a theory focused on one slice of experience or reality, the Ecology of Human Development looks more holistically at what is happening in the world. It takes into consideration even subtle, seemingly distant, influences realizing that such events might impact development in substantive ways. It is a multidisciplinary approach for understanding human development.

The theory was developed by Urie Bronfenbrenner. He was born in Moscow in 1917, and his family immigrated to the United States when he was six years old. He studied psychology as an undergraduate student at Cornell and later went on to gain a master's degree in developmental psychology from Harvard and a doctorate from the University of Michigan. He held various positions in his career, the last and longest stint as a professor at Cornell. It was in this role where he continued his research and published the book *The Ecology of Human Development: Experiments by Nature and Design* (1979). Bronfenbrenner was passionate about integrating developmental research findings into policies and work practices. This led him to be a cocreator of the Head Start program in the United States. He also frequently counseled presidents and vice presidents on domestic policy and CEOs on the importance of family issues (Ceci 2006, 174). Although his name is not widely recognized by the general public, his influence in the fields of education and psychology have been far-reaching because his "ecological approach to human development shattered barriers among the social sciences and forged bridges among the disciplines" (ibid., 173).

Bronfenbrenner believed that human development takes place within "a set of nested structures" (1979, 3). The first such structure is the microsystem. It is defined as "a pattern of activities, roles, and interpersonal relations experienced by the developing person in a given setting with particular physical and material characteristics" (ibid., 22). It is personal, tangible, and experiential. Each cross-cultural ministry partner is involved in multiple microsystems. For instance, a person's family is one system; church friends would be another microsystem. Each microsystem influences a person's development and perceptions about the world.

The second is the mesosystem. It "comprises the interrelations among two or more settings in which the developing person actively participates" (ibid., 25). Whereas a microsystem is one small group that influences a person's expectations, the mesosystem reflects various groups shaping a partner's development. For children a common mesosystem would be "relations among home, school, and neighborhood peer group; for an adult, among family, work, and social life." The mesosystem is made up of a group of microsystems. "It is formed or extended whenever the developing person moves into a new setting" (ibid.).

The third is the exosystem. It "refers to one or more settings that do not involve the developing person as an active participant, but in which events occur that affect, or are affected by, what happens in the setting containing the developing person" (ibid.). An example of this might be how missionaries in the Buddhist world are impacted when companies that employ their financial supporters decide to close down their factories or lay off personnel in their businesses. The missionaries will rarely know the executives who made such decisions but they are deeply impacted nonetheless. Public policy is in the realm of the exosystem.

Many people are never engaged in the process of crafting public policy, yet their lives are profoundly impacted by decisions made in that realm.

The fourth is the macrosystem. It relates to the consistencies found in the micro-, meso-, and exosystems "at the level of the subculture or the culture as a whole, along with any belief systems or ideology underlying such consistencies" (ibid., 26). The macrosystem forms the blueprint—the common image or thread that seems to be evident in each level within the macrosystem. Another way to describe this phenomenon would be to say that the DNA found in the macrosystem is also found in each of the continually smaller, nested systems. If the DNA or common thread is not present, there is probably a different macrosystem is at work.

## ILLUSTRATING THE ECOLOGY OF HUMAN DEVELOPMENT

Sometimes it helps to see a theory visually. Below is a simplified diagram designed to illustrate how the Ecology of Human Development might be impacting a partner coming from the United States:

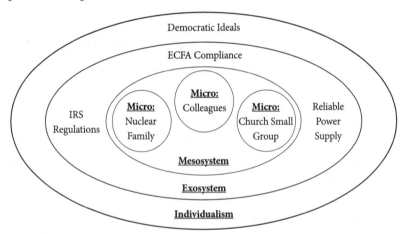

*FIGURE 1: BRONFENBRENNER AND CROSS-CULTURAL PARTNERSHIP*

Let's assume David is a new partner from the United States. He has just arrived in Sri Lanka where he hopes to partner with a few pastors in the region and also with a well-respected theological institution. David has been deeply influenced by his family. He is single and is in regular communication with his parents and siblings via Skype. His friends from his church small group pray for him regularly, and he confides in them when he gets discouraged. He also has close relationships with several of his colleagues at the home office of his sending agency.

David was raised in an urban area where there was always a reliable infrastructure, so he takes many things like electricity for granted. He knows there will be a funding component to the partnerships he hopes to establish. He is keenly aware that there must be good financial accountability so he and his mission can abide by standards set by the Internal Revenue Service. Also, since his mission was recently accepted as a member of the Evangelical Council for Financial Accountability, he feels additional responsibility to abide by their standards as well. Although he rarely expresses it, he deeply fears that if the partnerships he establishes in Sri Lanka cannot comply with these standards, it might ruin his professional reputation and make future ministry difficult. He carries with him, often subconsciously, democratic ideals of fairness and independence. David's story, though simplified, provides ample data for us to see how the Ecology of Human Development theory can be applied. Using this theory, we can begin to grasp and understand the interconnectedness and impact of the systems that influence David and that will continue to shape his expectations.

## MISSIOLOGICAL STRENGTHS AND WEAKNESSES

Bronfenbrenner's theory is a systems approach to human development, the core level being a small group of people in relationship. It is this very aspect of Bronfenbrenner's work that makes it so helpful for partners whose own cultures are individualistic. The theory forces mission practitioners to take into account the interconnectivity of human relationships. The Ecology of Human Development can also provide a helpful bridge for those who are prone to compartmentalized thinking. Bronfenbrenner's theory, which is holistic in nature, seems well suited to Buddhist contexts which tend to function from a holistic frame of reference.

There are, however, significant limitations in this theory if applied in partnerships seeking to foster new church-planting and evangelistic ministries. Bronfenbrenner's work does not account for the spiritual dimension of life. For many pastors, evangelists, and church planters engaged in cross-cultural partnerships in Buddhist countries, there is a deep concern for personal spiritual transformation. There is also a keen awareness that we battle not against flesh and blood but against powers and principalities (Eph 6:10–20). As such we recognize that it is not merely the systems that fashion behavior but invisible forces of good and evil at work in and through these very systems (2 Kgs 6:8–23; Dan 10:12–14).

Although the spiritual perspective is missing in the Ecology of Human Development, the theory as a whole provides a broader lens for expatriate missionaries working in Buddhist contexts and for the indigenous mission leaders partnering with them. Since many engaged in ministry partnerships have some level of theological training, most already understand the pressing need for prayer and intercession. When relationships begin to deteriorate, spiritual warfare is frequently cited as a key reason for the demise of a partnership. What mission leaders seem to be less sensitive to, or less able to navigate, are the inherent developmental differences which arise because of experiences within the various systems mentioned by Bronfenbrenner. Without greater awareness about the influence of these systems and without tools to navigate diversity, partnering in Buddhist cultures can be fraught with frustration and setbacks.

## HOW DOES EACH SYSTEM IMPACT PARTNERS' EXPECTATIONS ABOUT MONEY?

Understanding the micro-, meso-, exo-, and macrosystems can provide valuable insights regarding how ministry partners view money. Microsystems frequently provide clues as to many of the most tacit values and beliefs a partner will hold about money. Often these most deeply held values go unexamined. They are as imperceptible as the air we breathe, deeply influencing how we work while often remaining invisible and illusive. A look at how people apply Scripture provides an interesting example of the impact of these systems. Wealthier families and people shaped by individualistic cultures tend to emphasize passages about personal savings, personal responsibility, investing, and the need to plan for the future (Prov 13:22; Matt 25:1–30). People reared in collectivistic cultures have often been taught that it is wholly inappropriate to save and withhold money, especially if relatives and others in the community have pressing needs (Matt 6:19–34; Acts 2:41–47; Jas 2:14–17). Both value systems are rooted in the application of Scripture, yet they yield diverse expectations when they confront each other in a partnership. Another issue in the microsystem that shapes partners is whether there is an environment of plenty or a sense of limited good. These attitudes and influences are extremely powerful.

The mesosystem can also shed an intriguing light on partners' expectations about money in cross-cultural ministry partnerships. Are messages about money consistent in the various spheres? Do family members hold the same attitudes as work colleagues when it comes to finances? Are neighbors likely to think the same way as family members when it comes to money issues? If beliefs and attitudes about financial resources are consistent within a mesosystem, it will be far more challenging to work harmoniously with a partner who holds very different beliefs about these things. It is not impossible to partner together, but it will take far more time to build understanding and work through issues.

Earlier, a comparison was made that the youth pastor from Shanghai would likely enter a cross-cultural partnership with far different expectations than the older pastor from Myanmar. Such differences are logical given their different ages and nationalities. Obviously the impact of their microsystems and mesosytems are unique, even though both are from Buddhist contexts. However, even within the same country partners can be quite diverse depending on the impact of these systems. Imagine that Chanarong and Daw are two influential Thai Christian leaders. They are the same age. Yet Chanarong was raised in an affluent Christian family in Bangkok. His parents studied abroad in England. Two of his siblings live overseas, one in Canada and the other in the United States. Chanarong travels occasionally to visit them. He is involved in leading a large and influential congregation in Bangkok. Daw's microsystems and mesosystem are quite different. He is also from an influential Christian family, but his context is rooted in rural farming communities. Everyone in his family was raised in Thailand. No one has traveled abroad. The community he is from has suffered difficult times of flooding and civil unrest, but they weather each storm by supporting and helping one another.

Why is it important to understand each gentleman's microsystems and mesosystem? To enter partnerships assuming that all Thais will have the same expectations because they are from Buddhist contexts is unreasonable. For Daw it might be a sin to withhold financial resources from friends and family members if a health crisis arises. For Chanarong it might not be difficult to set aside donor-designated funds for a specific purpose as people within his mesosystem have many ways to address financial needs and emergencies. Both might be exceptional ministry partners, but they will surely enter collaboration with different expectations regarding how partners will relate to one another, how funds will be allocated, and so forth.

The exosystem frequently exerts incredible pressure on partners. Nowhere in the New Testament does it say Paul or any of the disciples formed a five- or seven-year partnership agreement. Yet most Christian mission organizations and many churches in places like the United States and Canada speak regularly of such agreements. They feel it is necessary to have them in writing. If it is not something illustrated in the New Testament, why is it so common in cross-cultural ministry partnerships? One reason for these agreements is that many countries have government regulations which require organizations to provide clear documentation for expenditures incurred in the course of ministry. If these are not adhered to, a ministry can lose tax-exempt status and funding can dry up overnight. Cross-cultural ministry partners facing this pressure will often refer to Romans 13:1–7. Other partners might face different challenges in their exosystem. Corruption within their own country's government might be such that if a ministry reports funding is coming in from other countries, their colleagues will face imminent danger. These partners will focus on a passage like Matthew 10:16 and urge their partners to be less naive. Much that happens in the exosystem will have significant implications for cross-cultural partners.

Finally, we consider Bronfenbrenner's macrosystem. Here are the broad issues where a subculture, culture, or overarching worldview are at work. Bronfenbrenner points out that wealth can function as a macrosystem. Wealthy people in one culture often have more in common with wealthy people in other cultures than they do with poorly resourced people in their own homeland. Jonathan Bonk's book *Missions and Money* (2006) gets at some of these issues. An example of this might be Chanarong. Although he is Thai, in some ways he might have more in common with wealthy people in Europe or North America than with people from poor farming communities in his own homeland. The same could be said of a struggling farmer from the American state of Alabama. That person might find it easier to partner with struggling farmers in Asia than with a Wall Street business mogul who has now turned his sights to philanthropy. Many engaged in cross-cultural church-planting or evangelistic partnerships in Buddhist countries believe their faith is the primary factor shaping their expectations. Religious beliefs can form a macrosystem. However, it is wise to engage in dialogue before assuming religious beliefs are the primary factor.

## WHAT IS DIALOGUE AND WHY IS IT SO IMPORTANT?

If Christian leaders are going to partner well in Buddhist contexts, it is imperative that we practice true dialogue. It is easy to make the mistake of assuming that if we are talking with people we are engaging in dialogue. However, true dialogue is so much more than talking. William Isaacs, founder of the Dialogue Project at MIT, writes that dialogue is "a *conversation with a center, not sides*" (1999, 19). David Bohm, a renowned physicist and theorist who is often quoted on the topic, explains that dialogue is "a *stream of meaning* flowing among and through us and between us. This will make possible a flow of meaning in the whole group, out of which may emerge some new understanding" (1996, 7).

Practitioners often confuse debate or discussion with dialogue. Debate, however, has a winner and a loser. Discussion often works in a similar way much "like a ping-pong game, where people are batting the ideas back and forth and the object of the game is to win or to get points for yourself" (ibid.). Isaacs writes:

> The intention of dialogue is to reach new understanding and, in doing so, to form a totally new basis from which to think and act. In dialogue, one not only solves problems, one *dis*solves them. We do not merely try to reach agreements, we try to create a context from which many new agreements might come. And we seek to uncover a base of shared meaning that can greatly help coordinate and align our actions with our values. (1999, 19)

In short, genuine dialogue changes us. It is a process of coming together, sharing deeply, suspending judgment, and listening without trying to prove or disprove your own opinion or position. In this process the whole of a situation can be brought into the open, and practitioners can begin to grasp their partner's experiences and context.

Why is dialogue so important to partnership? Although pastors and mission leaders engaged in a ministry partnership in a Buddhist context are Christians, it is highly unlikely that they will think and act alike. Their faith will shape some of their expectations, but so will things such as family relationships, work experiences, and economic policies. Many innate expectations which arise from our own contexts will not serve us well as we seek to collaborate across cultures. True dialogue provides space and a platform to get these ideas and expectations out in the open so everyone engaged in the partnership can have a shared understanding. And, from that place of shared understanding, dialogue enables us to go even further into a creative place where we can begin to form something new together which will serve us well into the future.

## DIALOGUE IN THE EARLIEST STAGES

Dialogue is essential in the most embryonic stages before a partnership is fully formed. Questions about vision are critical. If partners hold different visions about what partnership means and what they hope will be accomplished, it is important to discover this as soon as possible. It is imperative to take time at the beginning to dialogue about many issues. Queries such as the following are beneficial: What does partnership look like in your context? What are the characteristics of a good partner in your context? What are the characteristics or behaviors of a bad partner? What would we like to see happen in ministry? What can we do together that we cannot accomplish if we work separately? Cross-cultural collaboration is not easy. If we do not have a clear vision of what we hope to accomplish together and why it is so important, it can be difficult to persevere through the obstacles that will arise in the months and years ahead. Daniel Rickett's book *Making Your Partnership Work* (2002) is a good resource listing many questions to consider before actually forming a partnership.

Other factors such as leadership are important as each partner will likely have a different leadership style (Lingenfelter 2008; Plueddemann 2009). These types of queries can serve partners well: What does leading well look like in your context? Describe good leaders from your perspective. What are the characteristics of a bad leader? If we partner together, will we lead equally? Will we each take the lead in different spheres? In which areas is it better for you or your ministry to take the lead? In which areas is it better for me or my organization to lead?

In many cross-cultural partnerships the biggest arguments arise because of differing beliefs about how funds should be raised, spent, and accounted for (Lederleitner 2010b). If careful dialogue does not happen in the earliest stages of a partnership, collaboration will often end poorly. Partners need to carefully consider a number of questions about funding: What are the benefits of utilizing outside funding? What are the drawbacks or potential unintended consequences? In light of this, what portion should be raised locally and what additional amount, if any, should come from outside sources? If outside funding can at times lead to unhealthy dependency, how will we develop strategies from the beginning to lessen the likelihood of that happening?

In addition to issues related to outside funding and dependency, dialogue is also necessary when it comes to operational issues. How will funds be accounted for? What capacity is there to receipt and keep track of funds? Are there any complicating factors if funds are wired or sent in from other countries, such as danger to your colleagues? What type of reporting will best serve our partnership? Often different types of reporting are needed for different constituencies. For instance, what type of reporting would be most helpful to local or foreign donors? What type of reporting would be most helpful for colleagues actively engaged in the ministry? What type of reporting might be helpful for the community or people group we hope to reach or serve through this partnership? How will we know when our collaboration is no longer needed? And when the goals or outcomes of the partnership have been met, what steps or actions are best for us to take? We need to dialogue in such a way that we create processes that serve not only ourselves and our donors, but also make space and include the voices of the people our ministry is seeking to serve or help.

In this area of money and mission, Bronfenbrenner's Ecology of Human Development model can greatly assist partners in the dialogical process. As you consider each ring of influence, you can ask one another what unique expectations and pressures you face because of relationships with these various groups of people or spheres of influence. As stories are told, a shared content is built. All views can stand without needing to be defended or justified. The goal of dialogue is not to prove one experience or belief system is better or worse than another. The goal of dialogue is for partners to deeply understand and hear one another's perspectives. It is at this point, however, that partners need to face a sobering reality. Cross-cultural collaboration often means we have to take additional steps and go further than what our own culture requires. Partnering well across cultures means we need to create a new way of working together. If the partner with funding mandates all the processes and requirements, it is not partnership but neocolonialism (Lederleitner 2010a). Partnership requires the willingness of all parties to adapt and change so ministry can be done collaboratively in a way that honors and respects everyone involved.

## DIALOGUE THROUGHOUT THE PARTNERSHIP

In many ways it would be much easier if we could dialogue once about crucial issues, make decisions, and then work on autopilot from that point forward. However, that is not how things work. Often people change roles, and those continuing the partnership are not the same ones who started it. When this happens it is good to go back to the basics and revisit these questions and conversations with the new people working in the partnership. It is also beneficial to revisit these queries in an older or established partnership to provide a platform for deeper understanding.

It is inevitable that no matter how carefully we dialogue in the earliest stages of partnership formation, other areas that we had never considered will arise. Sometimes when an expectation is very deep, it unconsciously impacts how we see the world, and we are not even aware that it is at work within us until we become angry or frustrated about how something is being handled. Other times tensions might arise in our partnership because we say one thing and do another. "A dialogical approach requires that we learn to be aware of the contradictions between what we say and what we do" (Isaacs 1999, 29–30), because these create blocks in our relationships. "The very nature of such a 'block' is, however, that it is a kind of insensitivity or 'anesthesia' about one's own contradictions" (Bohm 1996, 5). If partnerships are going to function well, we need to find ways to dialogue not only in the most initial phases of partnership formation but throughout all phases of collaboration.

It is at this point that dialogue in a Buddhist country will likely deviate from the dialogical literature mentioned earlier. As we look at where the highest populations of Buddhists reside, as indicated earlier, we begin to realize that insights from the field of intercultural communication can also serve us well. Edward Hall, the person often referred to as the father of the field of intercultural communication, did extensive work in the Japanese context (1959, 1976). Hall explains that cultures are by nature low- or high-context. A low-context culture puts a great deal of emphasis on spoken and written words. In high-context cultures like Japan, people rely less upon words but more on the context and all the nonverbal forms of communication to discern how people are feeling and what they are thinking. If cross-cultural partners do not understand that a different form of communication might be at work in their relationships, it is easy for misunderstandings and conflicts to arise. Hall refers to this indirect and nonverbal form of communication as the silent language.

Often indirect or nonverbal communication is used as a means to preserve harmony and protect others from losing face. Sociologist David Yau-fai Ho writes, "While it is not a necessity for one to strive to gain face, losing face is a serious matter which will, in varying degrees, affect one's ability to function effectively in society" (1976, 867). Other times indirect or nonverbal communication is enacted because a partner has already lost face. Ho explains:

The possibility of losing face can arise not only from the individual's failure to meet his obligations but also from the failure of others to act in accordance with his expectations of them—that is, not only from the individual's own actions, but also from how he is treated by others. Moreover, the individual's face may be threatened by actions which are not aimed directly at him: a lack of deference shown by others to his friends, relatives, subordinates, for instance, could also be interpreted as depriving him of face. (ibid., 873)

"Conflict is a face-threatening process" (Ting-Toomey and Oetzel 2003, 138), and because of this, great care and forethought need to be invested in how to address conflict when partnering in Buddhist contexts. Duane Elmer's book *Cross-cultural Conflict* (1993) provides many helpful and creative suggestions about this issue. In many Buddhist contexts, using a third party to facilitate a continued sharing of expectations, feelings, and attitudes about sensitive issues is extremely beneficial for ongoing dialogue.

## CONCLUSION

Given the diversity present in Buddhist contexts, the Ecology of Human Development and dialogue are two tools which can help cross-cultural ministry partners better understand one another's expectations. This is especially important when it comes to financial matters. When expectations are not understood and respected, they undermine collaboration and trust (Lederleitner 2010a). Good relationships are always the best way to foster financial accountability, because people are more careful regarding funding if they care and understand how their actions will impact their partners. This is true whether partners are contributing funds or using them for ministry. Yet it is impossible to have truly good relationships if we do not understand the core beliefs that undergird our partners' expectations.

Bronfenbrenner's theory also espouses that human development is enhanced if people can work together in tasks with people outside their normal circles of influence (1979, 282–84). Perhaps God knows we will develop more fully if we partner with people from other cultures. Often with each cross-cultural relationship and collaborative effort we stretch and grow. We see the world in new ways, and our tacit assumptions and expectations are able to be brought to the surface so they can be scrutinized more intentionally. By understanding the circles of influence that fashion our partners' lives, we are able to grasp God's character in new ways. Dialogue is a critical factor in the process, as is learning to respect cultural differences that impact how dialogue functions in various contexts. Perhaps partnering together across cultures is part of God's plan as he readies us for the day when we will worship and serve him together for all eternity (Rev 5:9,10)!

# REFERENCES

Bohm, David. 1996. *On dialogue*. New York: Routledge.

Bonk, Jonathan. 2006. *Missions and money: Affluence as a missionary problem—revisited*. Maryknoll, NY: Orbis Books.

Bronfenbrenner, Urie. 1979. *The ecology of human development: Experiments by nature and design*. Cambridge: Harvard University Press.

Ceci, Stephen J. 2006. Urie Bronfenbrenner (1917–2005). *American Psychologist* 61, no. 2: 173–74.

Compare Infobase Limited. 2006. Maps of World. http://www.mapsofworld.com/world-top-ten/world-top-ten-countries-with-largest-buddhist-populations-map.html.

Elmer, Duane. 1993. *Cross-cultural conflict: Building relationships for effective ministry*. Downers Grove, IL: InterVarsity.

Gupta, Paul R., and Sherwood G. Lingenfelter. 2006. *Breaking tradition to accomplish vision: Training leaders for a church planting movement*. Winona Lake, IN: BMH Books.

Hall, Edward. 1959. *The silent language*. Greenwich, CT: Fawcett.

———. 1976. *Beyond culture*. New York: Anchor Books.

Ho, David Yau-fai. 1976. On the concept of face. *American Journal of Sociology* 81, no. 4: 867–84.

Isaacs, William. 1999. *Dialogue and the art of thinking together*. New York: Currency.

Lederleitner, Mary. 2010a. An approach to financial accountability in mission partnerships. In *Serving Jesus with integrity: Ethics and accountability in missions*, ed. Dwight Baker, 27–47. Pasadena: William Carey Library.

———. 2010b. *Cross-cultural partnerships: Navigating the complexities of money and mission*. Downers Grove, IL: InterVarsity.

Lingenfelter, Sherwood G. 2008. *Leading cross-culturally: Covenant relationships for effective Christian leadership*. Grand Rapids: Baker Academic.

Plueddemann, James E. 2009. *Leading across cultures: Effective ministry and mission in the global church*. Downers Grove, IL: IVP Academic.

Rickett, Daniel. 2002. *Making your partnership work*. Enumclaw, WA: WinePress.

Ting-Toomey, Stella, and John G. Oetzel. 2003. Cross-cultural face concerns and conflict styles: Current status and future directions. In *Cross-cultural and intercultural communication*, ed. William B. Gudykunst, 127–146. Thousand Oaks, CA: Sage.

# 6

## SPEAKING OF THE UNSPEAKABLE: MONEY AND MISSIONS IN PATRON-CLIENT BUDDHIST CULTURES

### Paul H. De Neui

Introductions within the Buddhist world of Asia follow a fairly predictable pattern of requisite questions. These include questions about names, country of origin, age (to determine appropriate honorific titles), occupation, and ultimately in some form the question, "How much money do you make?" When asked by certain individuals in specific contexts, some Asians might be offended by this question, but for the most part it is expected and socially acceptable. One's money or lack thereof is talked about all the time among people of the Buddhist world. But for most Westerners, and especially Christians, to talk of one's personal financial situation is to speak of the unspeakable. The average Westerner is very open about many highly personal issues that an Asian would never discuss in public, but when it comes to the topic of personal wealth, the invisible line into the private zone has been crossed. To ask how much money one makes is considered very rude in the West. Keeping one's personal financial information confidential is a widely held, unspoken rule. Some Western companies have even instituted policies prohibiting the discussion of salary specifics (Weiss 2010). With the exception of highly paid entertainment and sports figures, the majority of Westerners feel that personal wealth is a topic of conversation that is not merely uncomfortable but out of bounds. One author suggests that this may be due to the belief that people are paid according to their worth, and many do not wish this to be public knowledge (Wanning 2005, 226). In all other areas of life, intimate or otherwise, comparison is the norm for Westerners, but not on this subject. To talk of one's money is taboo.

But in the Buddhist world of Asia it is not uncommon to ask, "How much money do you make?" Asians ask these questions of each other frequently so why not ask the Westerner? Why is it that those (including Christians) from blatantly materialistic Western societies shy away from talking of money when those (including Christians) from Buddhist societies, where detachment from the material world is promoted, so eagerly and regularly discuss personal finance in detail at every level? One reason for this divergence is the differing perspectives on patron-client relationships. By failing to understand these differences, both Asian and Western co-workers in mission fail to move forward together in the Buddhist world. At the risk of offending both sides, this personal reflection attempts to raise awareness of a very touchy topic, recognizing that as much as we all would rather go that way, conflict avoidance is not the answer.

## WHAT IS MEANT BY "PATRON-CLIENT RELATIONSHIP"?

The terms "patron" and "client" originated when common plebians (*clientem*) were dependent upon patricians (*patronus*) for their welfare in Roman times (Marshall 1998). This relationship was mutually beneficial in that needs of clients were taken care of by the patron and the patrons were insured to stay in positions of status and power supported by the clients. In the Middle Ages this system was labeled "serfdom." Today in the Buddhist world there are several social structures that continue to reinforce patron-client relationships as lifelong obligations. These can be seen in the political structures of most countries in Buddhist societies (Ledgerwood n.d.; Scott 1972).

A patron-client relationship can be defined as "a mutually obligatory arrangement between an individual who has authority, social status, wealth, or some other personal resource (the patron) and another person who benefits from his or her support or influence (the client)" (Anthromorphemics n.d.). This social structure continues all over the world in various forms and is widely prevalent in the Buddhist world throughout Asia.

## HOW DOES BUDDHISM PROMOTE PATRON-CLIENT RELATIONSHIPS?

The confines of this paper do not allow for a full historic account of how Buddhism has incorporated and influenced patron-client relationships throughout Asia.

Many teachings of the Buddha encourage one to fulfill one's filial and social responsibilities. One important aspect of Buddhism, however, can be highlighted which builds into the worldview of the patron-client system and that is the importance of seeking a place of dependence or refuge to facilitate personal progress towards Buddhism's ultimate goal of nirvana. In Buddhism the self is the source of salvation. The Buddha taught that the individual, or oneself, was the proper place of dependence. Yet there are places of refuge for that individual— dependence in a variety of forms. From its historical context of origin up until the present time, Buddhism addresses and reinforces a patron-client relationship. The sacred *Triratana* (Triple Gems) of Buddhism are a provision primarily for refuge, as the ultimate place of human dependence. Variations of the vows of refuge are repeated in all forms of Buddhism in Pali, Sanskrit, or other languages:

> I take refuge in the Buddha.
> I take refuge in the Dharma.
> I take refuge in the Sangha.

Salvation in Buddhism is not found in a person, but refuge for the journey can be found in these three sources which ultimately aid the individual. Without them the individual cannot achieve freedom from the reincarnation that only brings more suffering. The three places of refuge are not ways out of this life, but rather through this life, and ultimately out of the cycle of suffering. The choice of dependence is upon the individual. Another analogy may be useful.

> The analogy of sickness is often used; Buddha is the doctor; Dharma is
> the medicine; Sangha is the nurse; we are the patient; the cure is taking
> the medicine, which means practising the methods. Taking refuge is
> like unpacking the medicine and deciding to follow the doctor's advice.
> (Harderwijk 2007)

The reality of a human patron-client relationship is established in Buddhism through taking refuge in Buddha and all those who are part of the Sangha, whether that includes the supreme leader (Dalai Lama), the ordained monk in the saffron robe (Theravada), or all of the community of the Buddhist faithful (Mahayana). Buddhist teaching promotes patron-client relationships in regards to highly honoring all of the Triple Gem and avoiding any shame that might fall on any part of it.

To show respect to the Buddha: respect all images of the Buddha, treat these as if they are Buddhas. Dharma: respect texts, treat them with utmost care. Sangha: respect even piece of robes and all who wear robes (despite behaviour). (ibid.)

## TWO VIEWS ON PATRON-CLIENT RELATIONSHIPS

There are two extremes of the patron-client issue that impact how mission is done in the Buddhist world. Money will be a major facilitator impacting the end results on both sides. Below is a diagram that attempts to illustrate some of the differences:

| **Asian Buddhist Culture** | **Western Non-Buddhist Culture** |
|---|---|
| Lifelong Voluntary Indebtedness | Personal Independence |
| Views the other as | Views the other as |
| "Uncaring, insensitive" | "Poor planner, immature" |

*FIGURE 2: CONTRASTING VIEWS ON PATRON-CLIENT RELATIONSHIPS*

To many independent-minded Western missionaries, the idea of seeking a new patron implies a level of personal immaturity. These would stress how local ministries need to support themselves. To some missionaries from the United States, locals asking for money may bring to mind the children's book about the bird that fell out of its nest. This little lost creature wanders around the neighborhood asking dogs, cows, trucks, and anything it encounters the same pitiful question, "Are you my mother?" (Eastman 1960). Needing a patron may seem to some Westerners like the pitiful bird that cannot yet fly on its own strength. If the local person would simply plan ahead, set some money aside, and save instead of spending everything, they would not have to "demean" themselves by "begging." Thus thinks the Westerner, and from this starting point many cultural misunderstandings begin.

In his book *African Friends and Money Matters*, David Maranz addresses some of the source of the conflict felt by Western missionaries. Although written for the context of Africa, similar issues are felt by those working in the Buddhist world of Asia. Maranz describes the difference between Westerners and non-Westerners in terms of macro- and microsolutions.

What is the fundamental economic consideration in African society? I would argue that it is acting to ensure the survival of family and kin. This is largely accomplished through sharing available resources. In the attempt to achieve this, one of the most common behavior patterns followed is to seek *microsolutions* to problems. A microsolution is an action that gives a person a tiny, immediate advantage over a competitor in a socially acceptable way. Perhaps this is the only behavior that is open to them because of their relative powerlessness and lack of resources ...

In contract, the Western ideal is to seek *macrosolutions* to problems. Drivers will inefficiently wait in line (or queue) or at a stop light, and buses will very seldom stop outside of the designated bus stops. They depend upon macrosolutions rather than seek a microadvantage. If the macrosystem does not work well in the West, which frequently it does not, drivers will loudly protest, call in the media, contact government officials, hold public demonstrations, or otherwise seek changes in the macrosystem. All the time they continue to wait impatiently in line, while the politicians debate what macrosolution to adopt and find the tax money to put it into place. (2001, 4, 9)

Westerners focus on the big picture (macro) and non-Westerners focus on the here and now (micro). Neither is necessarily incorrect, but both feel that theirs is the most culturally effective and appropriate response.

Coming from the macrosolution perspective, there is a foreboding of fear and entrapment that occurs inside the Western missionary when someone brings to them the dreaded request for money. They don't automatically feel honored, nor do they appreciate being approached as a potential patron. In fact, quite the opposite. The missionary knows that this small request is not as simple as it may seem. If the wrong response is made, it will lead to many other problems: a lineup of jealous locals at the door, an inevitable downward spiral of dependency, miscommunication of the real essence of the gospel, the ruination of the reputations of less generous missionary colleagues, possible accusations of abuse of mission funds by supporters back home, and ultimately personal failure. The local individual, through her or his cultural lens, may have interpreted all the friendly words and gestures of the missionary as invitations toward deepening the interpersonal relationship and views a simple request for a small amount of money as a microsolution in that general direction. Friends, as understood in that context, help out friends. But the Western missionary, unaware of all that she or he has miscommunicated, feels the request in a macroway with a potentially dangerous ripple effect of wide-ranging ramifications.

It is not uncommon, however, for those same missionaries to have convinced themselves that their churches and financial givers back home are something entirely different from what Asians are seeking when they look for a supportive patron or ask for a small loan. Missionaries feel they have "raised their own support," whereas when a national asks for money for a particular need it is perceived as begging and lack of careful planning. The Western missionary views the relationship with her or his supporters as task-oriented and not necessarily personal in nature. Other than sending newsletters and the occasional home-assignment church visits, this kind of money is basically depersonalized as something called "support." But when the Asian seeks financial assistance from someone, it is essentially because of the depth of the preexisting personal nature of the connection that even suggests venturing the question in the first place. In the Buddhist world of patron-client relationships, to be asked is to be honored. This automatically sets in motion a number of implications that are well understood from within the high-context culture of Asia where everything matters and follows a carefully prescribed and followed (yet completely unwritten) social script. This is the part to which the Western missionary from outside can remain clueless for years unless someone enlightens him or her. Even if an explanation is made, if the Westerner fails to respond in the prescribed manner, the missionary is considered cold and uncaring and unsuitable as a patron. And because money is such a popular topic in the Buddhist world of Asia, the missionary can rest assured that word of this reputation will quickly spread throughout the "target" community.

## HOW DOES MONEY IMPACT PATRON-CLIENT RELATIONSHIPS?

The saying that money makes the man is also true of women and all missionaries. Or to restate it, money makes a master more attractive. In certain contexts, there are cultural implications attached to personal wealth that lead one to conclude that asking, "How much money do you make?" can at times be an attempt to perceive whether or not the new relationship is worth considering as a new potential patron or a source for a microrequest. At times it is simply curiosity, but at other times it is exploratory of power.

A successful patron must be able to protect the client, care for the client, and serve the client. The client may never be able to repay the patron in legal tender or even in kind but instead will always remain faithful to the patron, give status and honor to the patron, defer to the patron, and seek to defend the honor and reputation of the patron. They may even recommend the patron to others, starting with invitations to mission events. The patron is the place of dependence. Without realizing it, many missionaries in the Buddhist world have become new patrons both to believers and those in the community. Is this a bad thing? Not necessarily, but it does have its dangers. Is it unbiblical? No, there are certainly examples of those who served to care for the needs of others in any way they could. Kings are obvious historic examples. The faithful priest, the godly prophet, the just judge, and the good rabbi are other cultural examples of patrons who were more than merely advisors or classroom teachers. Boaz, as a wealthy responsible citizen, exemplifies what Christopher Wright labels "the righteous rich," a God-honoring patron (Bonk 1991). Jesus sacrificially redefined the ultimate embodiment of patronage for all of us (John 12:23–33).

Western missionaries do have more money than many Asians. If they have not brought it with them in furnishings, fancy vehicles, and flat-screen televisions, surely it is held in a bank somewhere waiting for them. Whether this is actually true or not, it remains the widely spread, unspoken perception. The importance of perception in mission cannot be downplayed.

> It is of comparatively small importance how the missionary is maintained: it is of comparatively small importance how the finances of the Church are organized: what is of supreme importance is how these arrangements, whatever they may be, affect the minds of the people, and so promote, or hinder, the spread of the Gospel. (Allen 1962, 49)

If the missionary has no obvious local work for which she or he is paid, or no obvious source of income, there is a perception that someone somewhere is paying the bills. There is an overseas patron caring for the missionaries. To the marginalized in a Buddhist society, attaching themselves to the foreigner as a new patron to care for their needs may seem logical in order to move ahead or simply to survive. Missionaries are (and should be) eager to help, fully cognizant of the complex, lifelong responsibilities inherent in the role of patron assumed in the minds of those on the receiving end.

## An Example of Patron-client in Mission in the Buddhist World

The early Protestant missionary to Siam, Dr. Daniel McGilvary, is a prime example of the patron figure in mission in the Buddhist world. This pioneer and model of missions served in Chiang Mai from 1867 until his death in 1911. His original church building still stands on the east side of the River Ping in this city. McGilvary's role as the benefactor for the needy northern Thai, at that time referred to as the Lao, came in the form of new modern medicine such as quinine, through which miraculous healings and many subsequent Christian conversions occurred.

> McGilvary played the patron role well. He had combined the exalted statuses of teacher, healer, exemplary patron, and religious man all rolled into one. He did not hesitate to consult his own "patrons" in the form of the Bangkok authorities and to use the threat of such contact to gain advantage in a crisis. More important, he had a keen sense of obligations and empathy towards his clients. Due to their status and resources, most missionaries in this period would have been perceived as potential patrons by Thai, but few seem to have played the role as well as McGilvary. (Zehner 1987, 34)

While he remained the sole pioneer missionary and powerful patron, McGilvary fully fulfilled his responsibilities according to the Buddhist mindset. His following seemed to increase, and his influence spread. In many cases local believers transferred their relational allegiance to McGilvary instead of their other national leaders.

> Therefore, although Lao Christians remained under their formal obligations to Lao patrons, they had in McGilvary a new informal patron of potentially superior influence, and possessing the resources to give them some limited protections. In short, McGilvary had established himself as a new patron in Chiang Mai, capable of competing with the local patrons on at least equal terms. The mission's position and resources for playing the role of patron had increased, and they were in a position to provide an even wider range of personal services in a greater number of locations. (ibid., 33)

Later in his career other missionaries began to arrive and joined McGilvary's team, and a democratic system began to grow in the mission work in Chiang Mai. Coming from the West, new team members saw themselves as equals in a system that was organizationally flat. McGilvary no longer had the sole word on anything. He was part of a committee, and that committee made decisions. His power as a patron suddenly appeared very limited in the eyes of the local believing clientele.

This personal quality began to disappear, however, as the missionary force grew. The expanded core of missionaries in effect interposed itself between the local Thai leaders and their patron McGilvary. In effect, the new foreigners displaced the Thai from his innermost entourage, although not even McGilvary would have read the situation in those terms. Furthermore, because of the relatively egalitarian democratic processes by which the mission conducted its day-to-day business, McGilvary no longer dominated sufficiently to produce the policy exceptions and modifications that a traditional patron would have produced at will in his organization. (ibid., 38)

As is often the case, it was the issue of money that led to major conflict in the McGilvary mission. According to one analyst:

A cluster of internal disputes came to a head in 1895 over issues affecting the Thai, such as financial support. McGilvary favoured a combination of both mission and church support for the pastors and opposed sharp cuts in pay to the Thai ministers. Had the mission been run on the Thai pattern, McGilvary's prestige as founder and senior member could well have caused his views to prevail, but in an American mission his voice was but one among many. Thus, as the mission expanded, missionaries displaced local Thai leaders from their place in the patron's entourage, demoted their place in the local congregation, and increasingly ignored their personal needs and interests as leaders to an extent that McGilvary would never have done. The overall long term effect was a stunting of the potential for church growth which could have been had the patrimonial structure been maintained. (Taylor 1997, 103)

In future years the transition from missionary to local leadership would bring another set of problems. As Roland Allen warned, large mission compounds with missionary leadership in control "make it very difficult for any native to succeed to the place of a European missionary" (1962, 57). At that time the benefits of being related to that particular patron no longer applied, and the Siamese Lao went elsewhere to find a new benefactor, such being the nature of the patron-client relationship in many parts of the Buddhist world.

> The Thai will uphold this material interdependence only as long as it serves to benefit both sides. The Thais believe that the determination of a person's status in the social hierarchical order is dependent upon a composite quality called "merit" (Bun) or "virtue" (Khwaam-dii) ... They can expect such visible evidence of their good *Karma* such as wealth or pleasure ... This obligation or loyalty will exist as long as there are mutual benefits; as long as the patron is viewed as possessing greater merits. However, if the patron should suffer misfortune, this would indicate that her/his merit is insufficient, or that her/his *Baap* (sin) has now overcome her/his *Bun* (merits). S/he is, therefore, no longer dependable, so her/his client withdraws. (Ukosakul 1993, 142–44)

## A Contemporary Example of Impact of Money on Patron-client Relations

Not every inquiry, "How much money do you make?" is a request for new patronage. At times it may be, and at other times it may not. A client may fawn, flatter, and grovel to gain the favor of a patron, but the results are only shown in the attitude towards the client expressed by the patron. Financial success is an undeniable factor enhancing a potential patron's popularity. One researcher has shown that Buddhists in economic difficulties had more "money consciousness" (desire for more money) than those from high incomes. Both, however, were willing to accept jobs that violated the Five Precepts of Buddhism if the price was right (Ariyabuddhiphongs 2007, 43).

In Thailand, for example, there are many stories of Buddhist monks who preach against the purchase of lottery tickets. They attempt to explain how buying lottery tickets merely increases personal desire and discontent and only leads to more suffering. Yet many rural and urban Buddhist temples in Thailand will be very busy on the day directly preceding the announcement of the lottery scores. Dozens of otherwise unaffiliated or nonreligious devotees visit Buddhist temples on those days seeking advice and requests for winning lottery numbers from their favorite priest. If verbal advice is not forthcoming, they come to seek any auspicious markings or shadows seen on the sacred grounds of the temple, perhaps designs in tree bark or a number ascertained from shared stories, dreams, and visions. Anything could serve as a potential clue. The abbot of one Buddhist temple with which we were working in a community project refused to give out numbers for the lottery. He wholeheartedly preached against it. At the time, we were raising funds for a home for the HIV-positive that would be built on the temple grounds. Instead of giving out lottery numbers, this Buddhist monk would ask a devotee who had come for lottery numbers vague questions such as their date of birth. If someone said, for example, the ninth of the month, the abbot would ask them to buy nine bags of cement and offer it to the temple. When they had returned with the required number, and if an audience still remained, he would then ask the next person what the production number was on a certain cement sack, which might end in the number five. He would then ask the next person to buy five wooden posts that were fifteen centimeters square. Meanwhile the attentive audience interpreting the message would immediately write down, "9-5-15," and with respectful bows leave to go buy lottery tickets. Once one person was successful, the word quickly spread, and more would appear at the temple the following fortnight. Through this means, the home for the HIV-positive was built with both materials and additional financial donations of gratitude given back to the temple, and never a word spoken about numbers for the lottery.

What does this mean for the missionary or the local missionary working within the Buddhist context? Again, the insights from Africa can speak to the context of Asia as well:

> The Western quest for macrosolutions has led to the innovative and economically successful entrepreneur, the big business deal, the big merger, the giant international corporation, and other large systems that are economically efficient. They reflect Western ideals and means of building wealth and producing material goods and services. Bill Gates and Ross Perot, who have been geniuses at harnessing the system to their personal profit, are idealized men in this society.

> Who are the ideal citizens in Africa? They are the men who have political and religious power, social position, status and commanding personalities. In traditional African societies, they were also men who generously *shared* their wealth with their fellows ... Traditionally, chiefs lived at the economic level of their fellow citizens because they gave away

their wealth as fast as it came to them. They had high social position, but economically were on a level only a little above that of their subjects ... Present-day leaders in Africa who are unable or unwilling to distribute economic benefits to their followers have difficulties in maintaining their leadership and authority and retaining their followers. (Maranz 2001, 8)

Christ-following missionaries working in Asia would do well to review leadership styles of truly effective social innovators in the Buddhist world. It can clearly be seen that those who are most influential not only use their economic means to advance their patron status but have also gained the trust and respect of those whom they seek to serve. Personal wealth may be one initial factor determining a potential patron and how she or he is viewed in the society; however, it is the attitude toward and use of a patron's wealth, resources, and knowledge that communicates even more than the actual or perceived amount of money that the patron possesses.

## IMPLICATIONS OF PATRON-CLIENT FOR MISSION IN THE BUDDHIST WORLD

Comparing differing cultural attitudes toward money and how it impacts patron-client relationships in the Buddhist world remains simply an intriguing anthropological exercise unless some of these implications can be applied to God's mission in this unique context. Not every missionary is called to nor should consider taking on the role of the patron in a new society. In this chapter I would like to suggest several implications. First, those involved in mission in the Buddhist world need to begin by acknowledging the existence of the social structures in which God has called them to serve and recognize that this is primarily patron-client. This is inherently neither good nor bad; it is simply a cultural reality. It may not be the missionary's preferred form of relational structure, and that will remain a challenge as long as the missionary views the system as inherently wrong. Within every human culture there are aspects in which God is glorified and other aspects in which humanity is glorified. Wherever humans are glorified, God is not, and this is idolatry. Wherever there are humans, there is the image of God, and in that same place there is the imprint of fallen humanity. Nowhere after the record of creation do we have any biblical examples of God simply affirming human culture as very good as it is. Instead we see God entering into human culture from Genesis 15 to Revelation 22 with the forms, systems, and languages to which humans can respond, and from there God moving the human audience to deeper levels of transformation. God does not destroy human cultures but rather enters them and redeems them from within. God is present in the patron-client system. The missional implications of this are that both the missionary's culture and the receptor culture are places where God can be glorified and are both places in need of God's transforming work. A patron-client system can be God honoring, as can be seen in the fact that most of the cultures in the Bible are patron-client in orientation. This is difficult for most Western missionaries to understand. Other social systems also honor God in their own ways, and both are in need of God's transforming work from within. This must include the home culture of the missionary as well the cultures of the Buddhist world.

Secondly, if we as Westerners are to continue to partner with God's mission in the Buddhist world, we must break the silence on personal wealth. We must begin to speak of the unspeakable. We must prepare ourselves for the uncomfortable questions that will inevitably come. This does not mean bragging or throwing out information carelessly. We must recognize that denial of personal wealth and privilege as a Western missionary working in the Buddhist world is a false and futile effort. Local people know more about us than we ever imagined! Those in the business world are taught to downplay the difference by explaining the difference in purchasing power at home and abroad (Hinkelman 1995, 163). But such attempts are seen for what they are—avoidance.

It is time to be honest with those whom God has placed with us as colleagues and partners in mission in the Buddhist context and find out how best to approach this difficult subject together. This threatens the very highly valued Western cultural norm of privacy, but that is a small price to pay for participating in the most important task one could have on this earth. The Western missionary must face the fact that talking about personal wealth is a painful process. He or she must be willing to be vulnerable to the co-workers with whom she or he is working, assuming that viable, long-term, strategic partnership is a goal from the outset.

Both those from patron-client and non-patron-client cultures can learn something from each other. Both positions can be supported from Scripture. Both cultures are in need of transformation. The Asian from a Buddhist culture will need to learn that complete dependency on anyone other than God is idolatry. The Western missionary will need to recognize the reality that total self-independence is also idolatry and must change accordingly. The scriptural model of the master who serves others, the body that is interdependent, and the increased responsibilities of those who have been given much are all part of a biblical missiology that must be implemented before Westerners can continue to partner well. Missionaries must be freed from their fears of a potential mistaken macrosolution, and nationals must be freed from their dependence only upon microsolutions. Both must learn that funding is neither the answer nor the limit to everything, and that all possess a variety of valuable resources that contribute to mutual enrichment and kingdom advance.

It is perhaps reassuring to know that even those clients who followed the most qualified patron in all of Scripture were not without their struggles and misunderstandings. Even with the utmost of cultural fluency, Jesus himself was unable to avoid the challenges inherent in the patron-client relationship regarding issues with which we still struggle today. In the midst of what we often read as one of the most sacred moments at the end of our Savior's earthly life, the Last Supper, there is recorded for our benefit an argument about loyalty, money, and power:

> A dispute also arose among [the disciples] as to which of them was considered to be greatest. Jesus said to them, "The kings of the Gentiles lord it over them; and those who exercise authority over them call themselves Benefactors. But you are not to be like that. Instead, the greatest among you should be like the youngest, and the one who rules like the one who serves. For who is greater, the one who is at the table or the one who serves? Is it not the one who is at the table? But I am among you as one who serves. (Luke 22:24–27)

Who are our benefactors in mission in the Buddhist world today? There is a role for outsiders whom God has gifted with money and other abilities, and there is a role for insiders whom God has richly gifted with cultural insight and a multitude of talents. All of us must ask each other in love as we work to partner together in mission, "Where is our ultimate place of dependence in kingdom activity?" The popular worldly models are still clearly seen, and we must confess how easily influenced we all are by them. The words of Jesus are just as true today, "You are not to be like that."

# REFERENCES

Allen, Roland. 1962. *Missionary methods: St. Paul's or ours?* Grand Rapids: Eerdmans.

Anthromorphemics. n.d. Patron client relationship. Webref.org. http://www.webref.org/anthropology/p/patron_client_relationship.htm.

Ariyabuddhiphongs, Vanchai. 2007. Money consciousness and the tendency to violate the five precepts among Thai Buddhists. *International Journal for the Psychology of Religion* 17, no. 1: 37–45.

Bonk, Jonathan. 1991. *Missions and money.* Maryknoll, NY: Orbis Books.

Chinchen, Delbert. 1995. The patron-client system. *Evangelical Missions Quarterly* 31, no. 4 (October): 446–51.

Copestake, James G., Alyson Brody, Martin Greeley, and Katie Wright-Revolledo. 2005. *Money with a mission.* Vol. 1, Microfinance and Poverty Reduction. London: ITDG.

Eastman, P. D. 1960. *Are you my mother?* New York: Random House.

Eskridge, Larry, and Mark A. Noll, eds. 2000. *More money, more ministry: Money and evangelicals in recent North American history.* Grand Rapids: Eerdmans.

Experience Project. 2010. Is it extremely rude to ask someone how much money you make? Experience Project. http://www.experienceproject.com/question-answer/Is-It-Extremely-Rude-For-Someone-To-Ask-How-Much-Money-You-Make/16391.

Goodchild, Philip. 2009. *Theology of money.* Durham: Duke University Press.

Harderwijk, Rudy. 2007. Going for refuge. A View on Buddhism. http://viewonbuddhism.org/refuge.html.

Hinkelman, Edward G., ed. 1995. *Chinese business: The portable encyclopedia for doing business with China.* San Rafael, CA: World Trade.

Ledgerwood, Judy. n.d. Understanding Cambodia: Social hierarchy, patron-client relationships, and power. Center for Southeast Asian Studies, Northern Illinois University. http://www.seasite.niu.edu/khmer/ledgerwood/patrons.htm.

MacDonald, Jay. n.d. Don't be gauche: Polite ways to talk money. Bankrate.com. http://moneycentral.msn.com/content/savinganddebt/p122880.asp.

Maranz, David E. 2001. *African friends and money matters: Observations from Africa.* Dallas: SIL International.

Marshall, Gordon. 1998. Patron-client relationship. A Dictionary of Sociology, Encyclopedia.com. http://www.encyclopedia.com.

Mitchell, John P. n.d. Patrons and clients. Encyclopedia of Social Anthropology. http://www.bookrags.com/tandf/patrons-and-clients-1-tf/.

Rianto, Ratna. 2005. Millionaire missionaries' principles for giving. *Evangelical Missions Quarterly* 41, no. 4 (October): 466–71.

Saunders, Kenneth J. 1925. Buddhism and Christianity. *Expository Times* 37: 36.

Scott, James C. 1972. Patron-client politics and political change in Southeast Asia. *American Political Science Review* 66, no. 1 (March): 91–113.

Taylor, Stephan C. R. 1997. Patron-client relationships and the challenge for the Thai church. MCS thesis, Discipleship Training Centre, Singapore. http://www.pastegecko.com/Steve/MCS%20Patron-Client%20Dissertation.pdf.

Ukosakul, Chaiyun. 1993. *A turn from the wheel to the Cross: Crucial considerations for discipling new Thai Christians.* ThM thesis, Regent College.

Wanning, Esther. 2005. *Culture shock! USA: A survival guide to customs and etiquette.* Singapore: Marshall Cavendish.

Weiss, Piper. 2010. Three rude money questions that pay to ask. Yahoo! Shine. http://shine.yahoo.com/event/financiallyfit/3-rude-money-questions-that-pay-to-ask-2385995/.

Zehner, Edwin. 1987. *Church growth and culturally appropriate leadership.* Pasadena: Fuller Theological Seminary.

# 7

# EFFECTIVE PARTNERSHIPS FOR CHURCH-MULTIPLICATION AND INSIDER MOVEMENTS

## David S. Lim

Recent works have highlighted the fact that in spite of good and noble intentions, much of "foreign aid," including (and perhaps mainly) those in missions, has contributed to worse situations, particularly the perpetuation of paternalism (for donors) and dependency (for donees) wherever such relationships occur (Schwartz 2007; Corbett and Fikkert 2009; Greer and Smith 2009; Rajendran 2010, 22–25; cf. Everist 1989). In political circles, foreign aid has corrupted governments, and enriched and empowered dictators, too (Easterly 2006; Moyo 2009; Wrong 2009)!

This article focuses on how this sad state of international, interchurch, and interagency relationships can be turned into effective partnerships, particularly in advancing the cause of "people movements" or "Christ-ward movements" in the Buddhist world and beyond. I share from my experiences both as receiver, mainly as a Filipino mission leader in relation to various expatriate missions, as well as a giver, mainly as an ethnic Chinese church leader in Southeast Asia and the president of a global school with extension programs in Southeast Asia.

## PROBLEM OF MISSIONS PARTNERSHIPS

Partnerships are formed whenever two or more parties decide to work together in projects that range from micro to mega. It often starts with friendship and networking between people who share a common interest or cause, and in our case, cross-cultural missions and national evangelization. These can eventually develop into formal relationships which usually seek to fulfill specific and time-bound goals for the benefit of the parties involved.

But mission partnerships have been problematic for most of mission history. One classic case involves the unintended result of the sacrificial ministry of Rachel Saint, the sister of one of the five missionaries martyred by the Waorani Indians in Ecuador in 1955. After her brother's tragic death, she had returned to spend the remainder of her life as a missionary among the Waorani. When Steve, the son of the martyred pilot Nate Saint, visited Ecuador in 1995 for the burial of his aunt, he discovered that the Waorani church elders were waiting for American resources to supply their needs as had always been provided in the past, including seeds for their farms and material to repair their church facilities. Instead of supplying perceived needs, he returned for a time to live among the Waorani to help them set up livelihood training and businesses able to sustain and develop their lives as a people connected with the outside world (Saint 2007).

The former head of India Missions Association (IMA), K. Rajendran has very recently called for "the missiology of self-dignity" as a solution to the dependency that prevails in Indian missions, which I observe to be characteristic of many fields, especially in the developing world. He notes accurately, which is worth quoting in full:

Many Indian and the two-thirds world missions have some what come to a place of self-governance. In terms of self propagation and self-funding there are many struggles. Propagation and funding are connected to each other in some ways.

Propagation is to do with the methodology used. The methodology of the proclamation is too traditional and too old in many ways. There is also a theological tint to it as the propagation is most often connected to "full-time," "called," theological degree holding professionals and "cross-cultural workers." Thus, anything beyond this boundary, people are not able to think. The paradigm of global people at our doorstep and Gospel to all people through the missional Christians does not yet make sense to the many church going Christians. Missional Christians are believers in Christ who believe that the work of the missions is not just for fulltime Christian workers but for every believer who follow

Christ. Thus each committed believer feel and work as missionaries in any area of work that God has kept them as teachers, doctors, artists, etc. The other theological tint is that gospel to only to the poor. Because of this tint, we do not have competent people who will reach out all peoples other than the poor and the downtrodden. As many Christians come from the poor or illiterate background, they tend to reach the same. Therefore the rich and the influential do not come to Christ. Even if they come to Christ they are only seen as the "senders" by contributing funds to the "full-time" workers to the "unreached" places. Very seldom they are asked to be the missionaries among their own class. Thus the church missed out the idea of every follower of Christ being a missionary—missional Christians.

Thus, whenever there is a need for funding the churches do not seem to have the source as many in the church are from the poor. Thus all appeal is to reach the poor and the marginalized. In the longer run, the Indian Christian workers continue to appeal funds from the Western or the economically developed nations. Many of these friends contribute liberally but more for the uplifting of the poor than to bring the Gospel to them. Also with funding comes many stipulation of how to spend the funds including the foreign methodology and foreign face of Christianity. Some Christian work has used this "opportunity" to give exaggerated reports and misuse of funds and not able to raise local funding and leadership.

[At] any conference anywhere in India or abroad it becomes impossible to gather the right kind of people because of the funding issues. Every gathering need travel subsidy and thus at times we get leaders who are not supposed to be there and also a tendency of man pleasing for the subsequent funding for the work in India. Many times it is done at the cost of dignity.

The theological issue here again is that fund generation through businesses are silently not welcomed in "the ministry." Often, thus the ministries tend to be dependent in external funding, more so from the West, Singapore, Malaysia, South Korea, America and so on. The meaning of all partnership boils down to how much fund could be extracted from the relationship. In the long run it breeds guilt ridden paternalistic and or controlling relationships. Dignity is out of the windows. In many global conferences it is openly announced fund for the "sponsored" candidates or for the "poor brethren." Some Indians cringe in this situation and some are happy to perpetuate the "poor brothers" syndrome. This has to change.

Therefore IMA has been advocating all mission organizations to become self-reliant with fund generations from their area or through businesses etc. It is heart warming to see members like the Great Commission Movement Trust in Gujarat encourages all people to have jobs/businesses/vocation even if he is a fulltime pastor. Their philosophy is that a vocation not only makes a person financially independent, gives dignity but also makes him/her become an acceptable member of a society. (2010, 23–24)

This paper agrees with all these analytical views and recommendations, so it proceeds to highlight the four alternative measures to enhance future mission partnerships: commonality of strategy, friendship of equals, empowerment of locals, and servanthood of expatriates.

## KEY SUBSTANCE: COMMONALITY OF STRATEGY

Above all, effective partnerships must start only with those who share the same strategy, and in the first few years be very strict about welcoming new partners. To overcome all the weaknesses mentioned above and to be most effective in reaching entire peoples and communities that will finally put "closure" to fulfilling the Great Commission, this chapter highly recommends "church-multiplication movements" (CMM) or "people movements," particularly "insider movements" (IM), as the common mission strategy.

### Understanding Insider Movements

IM may be the best development from the "people movement" paradigm advocated by Donald McGavran's *Bridges of God* (1955) and *Understanding Church Growth* (1965) (cf. McGavran 1980). Through the influential Fuller School of World Mission (now called School of Intercultural Studies), three major mission strategies evolved among evangelical mission thinkers, mobilizers, and practitioners: (1) the "church growth" school, led by Peter Wagner, that promoted the megachurch model starting with David Yonggi Cho's Yoido Full Gospel Church; (2) the "saturation church planting" strategy, developed by Jim Montgomery from the Discipling A Whole Nation (DAWN) model in the Philippines; and (3) the "frontier missions" movement to target unreached people groups (UPG), promoted by Ralph Winter and the US Center for World Missions (USCWM) and enhanced by the concept of the "10/40 Window" by Luis Bush in the Lausanne II Conference in Manila (1989). It is through the "closure" vision highlighted in the Global Congress on World Evangelization (GCOWE) in Seoul (1995) that the search for the best strategy to finish the Great Commission was enhanced.

Subsequently, the concept of "church-planting movements" and later "church-multiplication movements" (CMM) surfaced in the late 1990s (especially through the 1999 booklet that eventually became Garrison 2004). This phrase was developed to describe the phenomena of rapid saturation evangelization occurring in certain mission fields. At the same time, the "insider movement" (IM) concept developed from the discussion on contextualization of churches triggered by John Travis' article in *Evangelical Missions Quarterly* (EMQ) on the "C-1 to C-6 scale" (1998). IM advocates prefer the C-4 and C-5 "radical contextualization" approaches.

By IM we mean an indigenous people movement where entire communities and sectors of society are converted to become followers of Jesus Christ without having to separate from their community (Travis and Travis 2005). It is

any movement to faith in Christ where a) the gospel flows through preexisting communities and social networks and where b) believing families, as valid expressions of the Body of Christ, remain inside their socioreligious communities, retaining their identity as members of that community while living under the Lordship of Jesus Christ and the authority of the Bible. (Lewis 2007, 75)

From another perspective, IM is

a growing number of families, individuals, clans, and/or friendship—webs becoming faithful disciples of Jesus within the culture of their people-group, including their religious culture. This faithful discipleship will express itself in culturally appropriate communities of believers who will also continue to live within as much of their culture, including the religious life of the culture, as is biblically faithful. The Holy Spirit, through the Word and through His people will also begin to transform His people and their culture, religious life, and worldview. (Higgins 2004, 156)

Paul De Neui has presented a schema by which to see what C-4 and C-5 Christ-centered movements would look like in a folk Buddhist context (2005).

## Missiological Assumptions of Insider Movements

The IM strategy includes at least six basic missiological assumptions of the mobilization of the whole church for spreading God's kingdom cross-culturally, as follows:

1. God intended his redemption plan to be spread to all nations (from Jerusalem) in the quickest possible time—for his desire is to save all (1 Tim 2:3–5; 2 Pet 3:9). And for this desire to be fulfilled, his plan of world evangelization must be quite simple; so simple that ordinary believers—including new, young, and/or illiterate believers—can do it, just like the mainly ordinary rural folks who became Jesus' original harvesters.

2. The gospel message is simple, too: "Jesus Christ is Lord who alone gives eternal life in heaven and abundant life on earth," which any believer can share immediately with others. Another version is: "Jesus loves me (or better, all) this I know, for the Bible tells me so." In Buddhist contexts, they may begin with the view that Jesus is the Light that Buddha saw when he was enlightened, or the Maitreya Buddha whom he predicted would come after him, or the fulfillment of the Four Noble Truths, Eight-fold Path, and Five Precepts. Then as they read and reflect on Scriptures, they will develop new insights into the lordship of Jesus in their lives and in the universe.

3. The quickest way possible is to mobilize as many believers as possible (if possible, every Christ follower), perhaps by the millions, to evangelize and

disciple the nations! The Great Commission is given to all believers. This is the priesthood of every believer in live action. Fung rightly observes:

> The spreading of the gospel in the early church period was not dependent on charismatic leaders nor any grand strategies of the established Jerusalem Church, but by the nameless, "powerless" people who acknowledged the Lordship of Christ and experienced the power of the Spirit (Acts 11:19). (2010, 1)

4. It is possible to plant and program the right DNA into new converts, as well as structure the right DNA into church life, so that they will grow and develop into missional, reproducing disciple makers for the rest of their lives. This consists of learning just three basic skills: (a) hearing God through prayerful meditation to turn his word (*logos*) into an application (*rhema*) to be obeyed; this discipline is also called *lectio divina*, the devotional use of Scripture; (b) leading a house or simple church in Bible reflection, whereby each one learns how to do "quiet time" (such as *lectio divina*) with fellow believers; and (c) friendship evangelism to share what they learn of God and his will with their networks of relatives and friends. This basic spirituality is enough to help anyone grow in the faith unto Christ-likeness for life.

5. These millions of reproducing believers can be produced through mentoring (or better, "discipling") by disciple makers, who are servant leaders who seek to equip all believers (cf. Eph 4:11–16) right in their regular, simple house-church meetings. Every Christ believer can be discipled to practice basic spirituality and share their faith in their own context without having to leave their community of residence, affiliation, or work.

6. These rapidly growing, multiplying groups of disciples or Christ followers can be called "church-planting movements" or "church-multiplication movements" (CMM), which aim to produce communal conversions and "people movements." If combined with community development and C-5 (high contextualization) approaches, they become "insider movements" (IM). Peoples can be converted *en masse* as we allow new converts to remain vital members of their families

and communities. "Fighting the religion-changing battle is the wrong battle" (Travis and Travis 2005, 13). The strategy is that of infiltration, to transform the people with the gospel from within their social structures, preferably without setting an alternative religious structure among them (Travis and Travis 2006)! Those who decide to follow Jesus become better Buddhists (and avoid being called "Christian" because of its foreign cultural baggage), and "converted" monks need not leave the Sangha, so as to make disciples from within their culture. Is this being deceptive? Not if we believe sincerely in our heart and conscience that the beliefs and practices that we adopt are not unbiblical or even good and pleasing to God (cf. Lim 2010b).

Thus CMMs and IMs are best seen in contrast to the "extraction evangelism" of the "imperial" approach (or "missions by wealth and power"), which has been the predominant "top-down" paradigm of Christendom missions. Instead, CMM and IM use the "friendship (or relational) evangelism" of the "incarnational" approach (or "missions by love and good works"). The best "bottom-up" practices are the integration of CMM (most effectively through house-church networks) (cf. Simson 2001; Zdero 2004; Lim 2010b), critical or radical contextualization of the gospel message (cf. Richardson 1981; Davis 1993; Lim 2003, 2010b) and church forms (cf. Kraft 1979, 2005; Lim 2010a, 2011; Richard 1999; Hoefer 2001), as well as community development and organizing (Lim 1992, 20) through lay (or tentmaker) missionaries, especially businesspeople and social entrepreneurs (Bornstein 2003; Rundle 2003; Wall 2005).

## Current Status of Insider Movements

The year 2010 may be the "breakthrough year" for IM. Although there was some hesitation in a plenary session at Tokyo 2010, it was fully endorsed in the concluding sermon by David J. Cho (perhaps Asia's Ralph Winter)—the Korean founder of Asia Missions Association (AMA) and the Third World Missions Alliance (which cohosted Tokyo 2010)—at the Tenth AMA Triennial Convention held in Jakarta November 3–7, 2010. In the past decade, IM has been gradually accepted by Western missions, and lately by a few Korean missions, yet numerous objections to it have kept it from being recognized by the mainstream of evangelical missions.

There are many success stories of CMM over the years, especially through the house-church movements in China and India. Mainstream missions who have done CMM in the 10/40 Window in the past two decades have gradually been recognized. Those who do IM are mainly those who work among Muslims (Garrison 2004; Travis 1998; Travis and Travis 2006) and Hindus (Richard 1999; Hoefer 2001). Fewer, yet significant CMMs have been reported among Buddhist peoples, especially in China (Deng 2005; Garrison 2004; Wesley 2004) and Cambodia (Carlton 2000), as well as some IMs in China and Myanmar (undocumented yet).

Recently a pastor in a restricted country told me that he is ready to launch an IM with a Buddhist family there. He has been trying to multiply cell groups among non-Christians, and in this ministry a Buddhist woman was converted to Christ on her deathbed. She instructed her family that Christians should lead in her wakes and funeral services. Five of her household were converted and will soon be discipled to start house churches among their own people—without having to affiliate with an established local church. This family's love gift to the pastor was God's provision for him to participate in the aforementioned AMA convention in Jakarta.

## Call for CMM and IM Partnerships

Given CMM and IM's present minority status and their unique and potentially fruitful missiological understanding and missionary approach, sharing a common mission strategy becomes a very important requirement. Having a commonly owned vision, defined objectives, and a common focus or purpose are clearly listed among the "key principles" that make for effective collaborative partnerships (Butler 2006). Having partners who do not share the same strategy will delay, hinder, and often also detract the group from pursuing the mission and goal of the partnership. May there be a CMM partnership or preferably an IM partnership for every unreached Buddhist people and community in the next few years.

# KEY RELATIONSHIP: FRIENDSHIP OF EQUALS

Secondly, the very nature of CMM, especially IM, requires that all partners accept each other and relate to each other as friends and equals, even in the patron-client relational culture that prevails in most Buddhist contexts. This transformational relationship prevents the patron from becoming patronizing. From the start, the expatriate should avoid the patron role, but should rather build on local assets or resources, so as not to create dependency. In IM, upon entering a community, the outsider models a simple lifestyle by living dependently on the hospitality of the local people; specifically, a "person of peace" (cf. Luke 10:4–6). Friendship, mutuality, and community are established from the beginning.

As in all partnerships, and more importantly for IM, there must be trust, mutuality, understanding, compassion, and sometimes forgiveness. And as in all human relations, especially intimate ones, this is possible only through mutual listening. People want to be heard: "They want us to understand their intrinsic claims, their justice of being. They want justice from us. But we can give it to them only through love which listens … Listening love is the first step to justice in person-to-person encounters" (Ross 2010, 145).

In order to make partnerships grow, more being, more living, more listening, and less talking is needed of each partner.

> Only the very brave … dare … to go back to the helpless silence of being learners and listeners—"the holding of hands of the lovers"— from which deep communication may grow. Perhaps it is the one way of being together with others and with the Word in which we have no more foreign accent. (ibid., 145–46)

So here perhaps is a more compassionate, more human, and certainly more challenging way of defining involvement—by listening. In life, to listen is to become involved. Good listening requires humility, vulnerability, availability, receptivity, and patience. To be a good listener means to be willing to share in the lives of others—in other words, the first step toward being an authentic partner (ibid., 146).

Listening enhances the acceptance of genuine involvement by each one, a committal of oneself to the other partners in trust. This element of trust is foundational, as each partner entrusts the direction and programs of the partnership to the others. They must each respect the others' cultural way of being and doing. They must give up control and share the responsibility (ibid.). This is precisely what Bishop Azariah of India (one of the few non-Westerners at Edinburgh 1910) meant when he spoke in his plenary message on what was amiss in world missions in his day, and is still relevant in most missions today.

I do not plead for returning calls, handshakes, chairs, dinners and teas as such. I do on the other hand plead for all of them and more if they can be expressions of a friendly feeling, if these or anything else can be the outward proofs of a real willingness on the part of the foreign missionary to show that he is in the midst of the people to be to them not a lord and master but a brother and a friend ... We ask for love. Give us friends. (Oliphant, Anderson, and Ferrier 1910, 310)

Yet friendships must translate into "giving" in give-and-take relationships. "It belongs to the right of everyone whom we encounter to demand something from us." This is the essence of the "I-Thou" relationship. Gift exchange in a way that both partners practice giving and receiving in a spirit of mutual respect enriches the relationship. This giving may be as simple as acknowledging that the other whom we encounter is a person. This minimum of giving can lead toward a maximum of self-sacrifice if required. In terms of partnership, this means responsibility. To be in a partnership means to be committed to giving within the partnership and through it (Ross 2010, 146).

The situation is complicated by the reality of great disparities in material resources between partners (Funkschmidt 2002, 570). What do churches in the Global South have to give to those in the Global North? In most instances, those from the Global North have not been able to name what they receive from their "partnership." Western partners usually know what they have to give, but they "[do] not know as clearly what [they have] gone to receive. And that is where the trouble starts" (Spencer 2010, 150).

Trouble starts in part because the partners are, as a consequence of this inequity, unsure of their commitment to authentic partnership. "It is necessary for the church in the West to demonstrate that it is ready to receive what is offered; it is also important for our partners to know of that receptiveness" (Thomas 2003, 384). Put more bluntly, Amon Eddie Kasambala, a Zambian, critiqued partnership by asking, "What can one receive when one has been on the giving side for a very long time?" (Spencer 2010, 150).

So, how do we do this in a world (and in the missions community) that behaves differently—in a world rife with unequal power dynamics, in a world where the powerful are heard and the powerless are not, and where the wealthy can choose to give and the poor are forced to receive? In a recent reflection about the last of the Millennium Development Goals—to "create a global partnership"—Spencer wrote that Americans need "to allow ourselves to be needy too, to see in these goals a message to us. It may mean that, contrary to dominant American impulses, we are just quiet for awhile, we listen, we don't organize anything or do anything for 'them.'" We just are (ibid., 151).

Fung rightly cautions that this mentality can be Asian, too:

> I am concerned that we as Asians may be repeating the same mistake that our Western brethren might have committed in the past—that is, to equate economic and political power with advances in the spreading of the gospel. We continue to reinforce the notion that the spreading of the gospel is always from the powerful to the powerless, the haves to the have-nots. There is a sense of Asian triumphalism that makes me nervous. (2010, 4)

Discernment is required to address the neediness of all partners. For "true mutuality," the "fatal mistake" in relations between Global North and Global South churches was that our partnerships have historically involved "the same kind of 'commodities.'" Reciprocity was expressed in an exchange of the same commodities that those in the Global North already had in abundance. "Genuine reciprocity can only develop where the two respective partners do not receive the same as they have given." The purpose of partnerships is to serve the needs of each other. It is not an exchange (ibid., 152).

What do those from the Global North need that a partnership could provide? Most of these are intangibles: phrases like "global awareness," "a broadening experience of the world," "a sense of what it is to be a global," "a window on the world," and "an incarnational presence." And individuals and institutions in the Global South can offer these things in abundance. Sandra McCann, an Episcopalian serving at Msalato Theological College in Tanzania, observed that "what Tanzanians have to offer is an example of Christ-like hospitality and a rich worship experience and a living example of joy and deep faith in the midst of poverty." Grant LeMarquand points out significantly that students at Trinity Episcopal School for Ministry (Ambridge, Pennsylvania, USA) return home from global experiences "realizing that they are in a missional situation *here*." They have found a "new way of seeing *home*." The benefits flow from "expanded horizons" (ibid.).

But Mortimer Arias, formerly the president of Seminario Biblico Latinoamericano in Costa Rica, adds the caveat that mutuality requires those in the North "to be specifically careful not to use the rest of the world … for the sake of their global education." It is clear that "use" is the key word in this warning (ibid.). Indeed, without the mutual give-and-take friendship of equals, no mission partnership can endure or even exist with integrity and dignity.

## KEY OBJECTIVE: EMPOWERMENT OF LOCALS/NATIONALS

Thirdly, effective mission partnerships must result in the empowerment of locals or nationals. CMM and IM's goal is the realization of the kingdom of God (New Testament) or *shalom* (peace; Old Testament) in particular communities and sectors of society. These transformed or redeemed communities must be indigenous: self-governing, self-supporting, self-propagating, and self-theologizing as they express their faith in simple ways out of their love for God by the power of the Holy Spirit. They must be contextual (not foreign) and community-based (owned and managed by local people).

For this to happen, priority must be given to the development of local leaders who are also empowering or transformational. To be transformational, the whole community, and not just their leaders, must be directly involved in the planning process. Input and decisions must come from all the stakeholders rather than top-down leadership-determined outcomes. We may start with a leadership-initiated partnership, but the partners should explicitly create structures, committees, votes, and other opportunities to engage their whole constituencies (cf. Scheffler 2008, 261–70). Hence, short-term partnerships between small organizations involving "just enough" funding may be most efficient and effective.

Partnership is "close to the biblical notion of *koinonia*" (Funkschmidt 2002, 568). It is grounded in God's indwelling, a message of hospitality, of mutuality, of guest and host (Reissner 2001, 5). In this relationship, nonresidents must keep in mind that they are guests who offer the gift of enabling and empowerment. But it is the local persons and organizations who play hosts, who offer the gift of freedom and opportunity—for friendship and partnership (Spencer 2010, 151). Therefore, the local people should be the senior partners whose interests and even authority and control must have preeminence, no matter the contribution each has invested into the partnership.

This is the principle by which the missions of Jesus and Paul were conducted. They always left an empowered community that was truly indigenous and contextualized in self-governing, self-propagating, self-supporting, and self-theologizing. These community-based "house-church networks" were not dependent on external partners and resources, and their receiving of external help on occasion, usually during calamities and persecutions, were showcases of their interdependence in the single body, or better, between the branches of their Father's business (or better, his global group of microcompanies)!

In our age of globalization, financial sustainability and growth is needed for the long-term development of communities and nations. So some, if not most, of the budget for IM must be allotted to income generation and economic development. We should join cause-oriented groups to advocate for "simple (or green) lifestyles" and "fair trading" to slow down the overpowering "consumer society" of globalization. There are many who are now working for a new economic order called "solidarity economy," following the principles of jubilee in Leviticus 25. The bottom line for businesses must now be fourfold: not just profit, but also planet, people, and prayer (financial, ecological, social, and spiritual), as stated in the Lausanne Forum paper on "Business as Mission" (BAM) (Tunehag, McGee, and Plummer, 2004). Many Christian development organizations like World Vision, Tear Fund, and Christian Reformed World Relief Committee (CRWRC) have been doing "transformational development," which includes livelihood training, microcredit, and microenterprise development (Myers 1999; Fikkert 2005; Corbett and Fikkert 2009, 201–14; cf. Yunus 1999), as well as fair trade.

These efforts must focus on the organization of people-owned and self-managing community organizations and social enterprises, like cooperatives, mutual insurance firms, credit unions, etc. (Lim 1992, 15–18; Fikkert 2005). The wealth generated by the poor will lead to "lift" in their individual families, who will often move elsewhere, thereby hardly helping their community. Thus we need to set up cooperatives to help keep the wealth while also generating more wealth in the local community. And the best way for any locality to gain wealth is to provide for both local food sufficiency and appropriate technologization and industrialization.

Many effective missions have also invested in the economic and social "lift" of their converts through providing basic schooling and vocational training, even up to postgraduate education. These programs eventually became Christian colleges and universities. Theologically, establishing Bible schools or seminaries to produce "full-time workers" must be avoided, since this violates the "priesthood of all believers" and promotes the "clergy-laity dichotomy," thereby leading to the "sacred-secular divide" that has plagued Christendom. Practically, IM is realized most effectively through "ordinary" believers sharing their faith in their residential neighborhood or in their workplace. The biblical "work ethic" is clearly promoted. This also frees the church from spending money on maintenance of religious personnel and institutions. IMs envision Christians living out their faith in the structures of society without having to set up parallel Christian structures, transforming the world as salt, light, and yeast.

Providing scholarships for leadership development for national movements has been very empowering, too. My school, the Asian School of Development and Cross-cultural Studies (ASDECS) seeks to fast-track this leadership development process through offering secular graduate degree programs (with biblical spirituality integrated in the courses) for national leaders for the struggling nations of Asia and beyond. These provide the leadership, not just for the churches, but also for the communities, even their respective nations, and beyond. Moreover, since financial accountability is almost always involved, the capacity of the local financial office for stewarding and accounting of the incomes and expenditures has to be ensured and enhanced.

Actually IMs do not require major external funding, except for the travel expenses of the catalyst-worker, just as Jesus trained his disciples to do (cf. Luke 10:1–9). Fung rightly observes, "Over-giving and over-receiving often cripple the work of God. A pastor from China once said to me, 'We do not need money from the West. Money will divide the church in China'" (2010, 2). The corrupting influence of money (especially of having more than enough) is human and global (cross-cultural). Believing that the resources for God's harvest are in the harvest field, these bivocational missionaries need minimal external support. With just authentic work, study, business, or even tourist visas, they can catalyze IMs wherever they go. It is possible and highly effective to simply send out such workers into the global labor market as maids, cooks, welders, seamen, and other low-skilled jobs as tentmaker missionaries, as Filipino Christians have been doing strategically since 2001. Using businesspeople as "foreign investors" for BAM may even be a much more effective way.

Yet external funding is needed for partnerships on the ground for their community/people, most especially if they work among the poor and marginalized. With basic community-organizing skills, they can mobilize the poor communities to become self-sufficient and fast-track their economic development with bigger capitalization. This external aid enables them to gain excess income faster, not just for their communal life, but also for their capacity to contribute to relief and development challenges and to send out their own workers, who are going to be more effective to reach out to their neighbors with similar cultures.

For evangelicals, a central concern for IMs is the self-theologizing aspect. Who controls the theological development of the indigenous movement? Most helpful may be Andrew Walls' insight that it took at least a couple of centuries before the early church developed, through different doctrinal conflicts, what eventually became mainstream Christian Trinitarian theology. He has suggested that we must be patient to let each community reflect directly from Scripture in their context, perhaps for at least three generations (1997, 2002).

Walls identifies three stages in the process of transformation of biblical faith into the Greek thought world of subsequent Western Christendom. The first, missionary stage, was typified by Paul as he began to adapt Jewish vocabulary and forms to Hellenistic worldview, categories, and language. The second, convert stage, was represented by Justin Martyr who showed that Christ can inhabit the Greek world and work to transform it from within; "conversion" means to turn what is already there in a new direction, rather than substituting something new for something old. And the final, refiguration stage, was seen in Origen who grew up in the Christian faith and yet was reconciled to its pre-Christian inheritance, and was comfortable and not afraid of either.

This should give comfort and confidence most especially to indigenous peoples and those who speak minority dialects, who are usually considered "poor." They will not need to surrender their identity, worldview, and culture to follow a foreign Jesus. They can confidently reflect on God's word in their vernacular and let Jesus enter fully into their culture and specific subcultures. This is the confidence that we have in the infallible teaching authority of the Scriptures (*sola Scriptura!*) for our faith and its transforming power for our practice/lifestyle/culture. As Christ believers doing CMM or IM in the midst of religious and cultural pluralism, we only need to hold on to two absolutes: God and his word that reveals his plan in the creation-fall-redemption drama in Christ. We call on all our earthly contacts and all humanity to share in this pilgrimage to obey his will for our lives, each in their cultural and religious milieu.

Hence, to be truly effective, priority must be given to the native who understands the local culture and situation best. If finances are involved, they must be incorporated into the budget made in consultation with the local leadership. During and after deliberations, their preferences should be given primary consideration, their initiatives and programs encouraged and developed, and their best materials should be the ones produced and reproduced, rather than just the translation of those foreign produced, no matter how effective they may be elsewhere.

## KEY ATTITUDE: SERVANTHOOD OF EXPATRIATES

And lastly, besides being aware of being guests in a partnership, expatriates or nonresidents must also view themselves as servants. In most instances, those from the Global North assume leadership in any relationship, just because of their superiority of position, education, and wealth (whether in reality or in mere perception). This is often combined with their self-confident personality, if not assertive demeanor, and the culture of most Global South contexts where guests are given preferential treatment. Hence, this is actually a test of the spiritual maturity of the missionary in practicing servant leadership.

The issue of power distorts all the fine ideals and makes the practice of partnership difficult and demanding. It is difficult to have a truly mutual relationship when the two parties possess unequal power. But that is the reality of our world today. We know that money, resources, education, land, access to technology, ownership, and much more are unfairly and unequally distributed (Ross 2010, 148).

The model of the incarnation is helpful here. We can let go of our pride and power, our privilege and sense of entitlement, insofar as we empty ourselves following Christ's way depicted in Philippians 2. We seek to empty ourselves of our pride and ethnocentrism, our feelings of cultural, religious, and technological superiority, which blind and grip us all. We seek to empty ourselves of the need to initiate, control, dominate, impose, manipulate, and run ahead in partner relationships. We seek to empty ourselves of autonomy and independence.

In cases where finances are involved, IM partnerships require the expatriates to share willingly and cheerfully, without strings attached, while rightly demanding contextual forms of transparency and accountability. In the New Testament, *koinonia* denotes "partaking together in" or having a share; it stands for the privilege of participation.

> We are then, to seek first for the inward bond which holds the fellowship of Christ-followers together, which inward fellowship is then externally manifested by the life of fellowship, with its almsgiving, sharing of property and breaking of bread, which we find in the early chapters of the Acts of the Apostles. (Warren 1956, 48)

In passages where *koinonia* refers to the life of the Christian community, the partnership with other Christians is made explicit in the taking of collections on behalf of the needy (Rom 15:26; 2 Cor 8:4; 9:13): "all are equally involved, all have committed themselves to God in trust, all have a share in common responsibility, all recognize that they belong together, that if one member suffers, they all suffer, all have a liability for each" (ibid., 52).

Bosch writes about "victim-missionaries," who, "in contrast to exemplar-missionaries, lead people to freedom and community." Could we say the same of "victim-partners"? In 2 Corinthians 8, Paul teaches about "the validity of paradox, about a God who, in spite of being all-powerful became weak and vulnerable in his Son." We live in a relationship with a crucified God. Do we in our involvement with him and as his ambassadors live likewise? Koyama complained that too often Christian mission has exhibited a "crusading mind" rather than a "crucified mind" and that it suffers from a "teacher complex." What attitudes do we exhibit when we enter into partnership? Do we adopt a crusading mind and teacher mentality, or are we disciples and partners with crucified minds, giving up our rights, manifesting the courage to be weak—living the paradox of a crucified, almighty God? Victim-missionaries are not powerful and successful, nor are victim-partners. In this asymmetrical and uneven world, victim-partners will not create what has been described as "a relationship of controlling benefactors to irritated recipients of charity," in which recipients end up experiencing a complex mix of gratitude and resentment at the same time (Ross 2010, 147).

These insights about vulnerability and "victim-missionaries/partners" remind us to adopt an attitude of humility and of considering others better than ourselves (Phil 2:3,4). Such sensitivity is required of the strong so they may empower the weak. A related issue here is what the partners are seeking to share. Money, resources, education, land, technology, ownership, and power may be unfairly distributed and may lead to distorted exchanges. But as seen above, what else are we seeking to share? Stories, traditions, ancient knowledge and customs, inheritances, joy, kindness, goodness, beauty, sustainability, difference—these too are to be shared and can restore a balance where there may be uneven power dynamics (ibid.).

Moreover, this practice of humility, vulnerability, generosity, and servant leadership can serve as good modeling for the locals/nationals, too, and thus promote and perpetuate the way of Christ. Such incarnational and cruciform pattern of sharing sacrificially is the way to fill up the gaps, weaknesses, struggles, and sufferings in the body of Christ—in a truly interdependent mutuality of partaking in each other's spiritual and material gifts.

## CONCLUSION

Finances have been a dominant challenge to authentic mutuality, leading to problematic partnerships where economic resources are disparate. This is not going to change, even if much of the Global North is struggling financially since 2008. The task is to work through financial inequities in a manner that creates and sustains mutual and authentic partnerships (Spencer 2010, 153). Key to this is an analysis of power, for it is from a position of power that wealthier individuals and institutions, religious and secular, have historically abused relationships and misused partnerships.

This chapter has shown that mission partnerships can occur only if the parties involved work on the four mutual measures: commonality of vision, friendship of equals, empowerment of locals, and servanthood of expatriates. Such arrangements assume the sincerity of all partners to do effective mission together, and the willingness of each to plan, budget, and discuss all matters openly and honestly. Each is free to accept or not accept the terms of any agreement within the partnership. In this process of shared discernment, the ultimate decisions about programs and budgets belong to each partner, yet each must be committed to listen to and learn from one another as they consider what are needed to fulfill their mission (ibid.).

How long should partnerships be sustained? For as long as necessary; that is, until the mission has been achieved to the satisfaction of the partners. It is best to set time limits from the start, while leaving the dates flexible and allowing for renewals or extensions. Time limits free each partner from the unsatisfactory phenomenon of just letting the partnership quietly die. Rather, timetables encourage evaluation, and as critical an exercise as this may be for any specific activity, it needs to be undertaken for the relationship as well. With this periodic mutual discernment process, the partners may reach shared decisions about the future. Whether a partnership is renewed or ended, or even dissolved earlier than anticipated, partners should remain friends, seek possibilities to collaborate on other programs/projects and find opportunities to celebrate the relationship (Butler 2006). The quest for partnerships that result in effective missions deserves constant celebration.

# REFERENCES

Bornstein, David. 2003. *How to change the world: Social entrepreneurs and the power of new ideas.* Oxford: Oxford University Press.

Butler, Phillip. 2006. *Well connected: Releasing power, restoring hope through kingdom partnerships.* Monrovia, CA: Authentic Media and World Vision.

Carlton, R. Bruce. 2000. *Amazing grace: Lessons on church planting movements from Cambodia.* Chennai: Mission Education Books.

Corbett, Steve, and Brian Fikkert. 2009. *When helping hurts: How to alleviate poverty without hurting the poor … and yourself.* Chicago: Moody.

Davis, John R. 1993. *Poles apart? Contextualizing the gospel.* Bangkok: OMF.

De Neui, Paul. 2005. A typology of approaches to Thai folk Buddhists. In *Appropriate Christianity*, ed. Charles Kraft, 415–436. Pasadena: William Carey Library.

Deng, Zhaoming. 2005. Indigenous Chinese Pentecostal denominations. In *Asian and Pentecostal: The charismatic face of Christianity in Asia*, eds. Allan Anderson and Edmond Tang, 437–466. Oxford: Regnum Books International.

Easterly, William. 2006. *The white man's burden: Why the West's efforts to aid the rest have done so much ill and so little good.* New York: Penguin.

Everist, Norma C. 1989. Dependency hinders development: An exploration of receiving relationships. *Currents in Theology and Mission* 16 (October): 350–55.

Fikkert, Brian. 2005. Fostering informal savings and credit associations. In *Attacking poverty in the developing world: Christian practitioners and academics in collaboration*, eds. Judith Dean, Julie Schaffner, and Stephen Smith, 77–94. Monrovia, CA: World Vision and Authentic Media.

Fung, Patrick. 2010. Partnering in the body of Christ toward a new global equilibrium. Paper presented at the Lausanne Congress, July 29, Cape Town. http://conversation.lausanne.org/en/conversations/detail/10664.

Funkschmidt, Kai M. 2002. New models of mission relationship and partnership. *International Review of Mission* 91 (October): 565–72.

Garrison, David. 2004. *Church planting movements.* Midlothian, VA: WIGTake Resources.

George, Sherron Kay. 2004. *Called as partners in Christ's service: The practice of God's mission.* Louisville: Geneva.

Greer, Peter, and Phil Smith. 2009. *The poor will be glad: Joining the revolution to lift the world out of poverty.* Grand Rapids: Zondervan.

Higgins, Kevin. 2004. The key to insider movements: The "devoted's" of Acts. *International Journal of Frontier Missiology* 21, no. 4 (Winter): 156–60.

Hoefer, Herbert. 2001. *Churchless Christianity.* Pasadena: William Carey Library.

Johnson, C. Neal. 2009. *Business as mission: A comprehensive guide to theory and practice.* Downers Grove, IL: InterVarsity.

Kraft, Charles. 1979. *Christianity in cultures.* Maryknoll, NY: Orbis Books.

———. ed. 2005. *Appropriate Christianity.* Pasadena: William Carey Library.

Lee, Hong Jung. 2002. Beyond partnership, toward networking: A Korean reflection on partnership in the web of God's mission. *International Review of Mission* 91 (October): 577–80.

Lewis, Rebecca. 2007. Promoting movements to Christ within natural communities. *International Journal of Frontier Missiology* 24, no. 2 (Summer): 75–78.

Lim, David S. 1992. *Transforming communities: Biblical concepts on poverty and social justice.* Mandaluyong City, Philippines: OMF.

———. 2003. Towards a radical contextualization paradigm in evangelizing Buddhists. In *Sharing Jesus in the Buddhist world*, eds. David Lim and Steve Spaulding, 71–94. Pasadena: William Carey Library.

———. 2010a. Ancestor veneration and family conversion revisited. In *Family and faith in Asia: The missional impact of extended networks*, ed. Paul De Neui, 183–215. Pasadena: William Carey Library.

———. 2010b. Catalyzing "insider movements" in Buddhist contexts. In *Family and faith in Asia: The missional impact of social networks*, ed. Paul De Neui, 31–46. Pasadena: William Carey Library.

———. 2011. Suffering (dukkha) as a bridge to evangelizing Buddhists. In *Suffering: Christian reflections on Buddhist dukkha*, ed. Paul De Neui, 77–92. Pasadena: William Carey Library.

Little, Christopher. 2005. *Mission in the way of Paul.* New York: Peter Lang.

Lupton, Robert D. 2007. *Compassion, justice, and the Christian life: Rethinking ministry to the poor.* Ventura: Gospel Light.

Marsh, Colin. 2003. Partnership in mission: To send or to share? *International Review of Mission* 92 (July): 366–72.

McGavran, Donald. 1955. *The bridges of God.* Eugene, OR: Wipf and Stock.

———. 1965. *Understanding church growth.* Grand Rapids, MI: Eerdmans.

———. 1980. Foreword to *A people reborn*, by Christian Keysser. Pasadena: William Carey Library.

Moyo, Dambisa. 2009. *Dead aid.* New York: Farrar, Straus, & Giroux.

Myers, Bryant. 1999. *Walking with the poor.* Maryknoll, NY: Orbis Books.

Oliphant, Anderson, and Ferrier. 1910. *The history and records of the conference.* New York: Revell.

Rajendran, K. 2010. IMA and its missiology over the years. *Indian Missions* (July–September): 8–25.

Reissner, Anne. 2001. The dance of partnership: A theological reflection. *Missiology* 29, no. 1 (January): 3–10.

Richard, Herbert. 1999. *Following Jesus in the Hindu context.* Pasadena: William Carey Library.

Richardson, Don. 1981. *Eternity in their hearts.* Ventura, CA: Regal Books.

Rickett, Daniel. 2001. Seven mistakes partners make and how to avoid them. *Evangelical Mission Quarterly* 37, no. 3 (July): 314–19.

Ross, Cathy. 2010. The theology of partnership. *International Bulletin of Missionary Research* 34, no. 3 (July): 145–49.

Rundle, Steven L. 2000. Ministry, profits, and the schizophrenic tentmaker. *Evangelical Missions Quarterly* 36, no. 3 (July): 292–300.

———. 2003. Preparing the next generation of kingdom entrepreneurs. In *On kingdom business: Transforming missions through entrepreneurial strategies*, eds. Tetsunao Yamamori and Kenneth A. Eldred, 225–44. Wheaton, IL: Crossway Books.

———. Rundle, Steven L. and Tom Steffen. 2003. *Great commission companies.* Downers Grove, IL: InterVarsity.

Sachs, Jeffrey. 2005. *The end of poverty: Economic possibilities for our time.* New York: Penguin.

Saint, Steve. 2007. *End of the spear.* Carol Stream, IL: Tyndale House.

Scheffler, Marcia. 2008. Partnership and participation in a Northern church–Southern church relationship. *Transformation* 25, no. 4 (October): 255–72.

Schwartz, Glenn. 2007. *When charity destroys dignity: Overcoming unhealthy dependency in the Christian movement.* Lancaster, PA: World Mission Associates.

Simson, Wolfgang. 2001. *Houses that change the world.* Carlisle, UK: Paternoster.

Spencer, Leon. 2010. Not yet there: Seminaries and the challenge of partnership. *International Bulletin of Missionary Research* 34, no. 3 (July): 150–54.

Thomas, Philip. 2003. How can Western Christians learn from partners in the world church?" *International Review of Mission* 92 (July): 380–85.

Travis, John. 1998. Must all Muslims leave Islam to follow Jesus? *Evangelical Missions Quarterly* 34, no. 4 (October): 411–15.

Travis, John, and Anna Travis. 2005. Contextualization among Muslims, Hindus, and Buddhists: A focus on "insider movements." *Mission Frontiers*, September–October. http://www.missionfrontiers.org/issue/article/contextualization-among-hindus-muslims-and-buddhists.

———. 2006. Maximizing the Bible! Glimpses from our context. *Mission Frontiers*, January–February. http://www.missionfrontiers.org/issue/article/maximizing-the-bible.

Tunehag, Mats, Wayne McGee, and Josie Plummer, eds. 2004. Business as mission. Paper presented at the Forum for World Evangelization, September 29 to October 5, Pattaya, Thailand. http://www.lausanne.org/docs/2004forum/LOP59_IG30.pdf.

Wall, Molly. 2005. Learning from a new wave of social entrepreneurs. *Mission Frontiers*, September–October. http://www.missionfrontiers.org/issue/article/learning-from-a-new-wave-of-social-entrepreneurs.

Walls, Andrew. 1997. Old Athens and new Jerusalem: Some signposts for Christian scholarship in the early history of mission studies. *International Bulletin of Mission Research* 21 (October): 146–53.

———. 2002. *The cross-cultural process in Christian history: Studies in the transmission and appropriation of faith.* Maryknoll, NY: Orbis Books.

Warren, Max. 1956. *Partnership: The study of an idea.* London: SCM.

Wesley, Luke. 2004. Is the Chinese church predominantly Pentecostal? *Asian Journal of Pentecostal Studies* 7, no. 2 (July): 225–54.

Wrong, Michaela. 2009. *It's our turn to eat: The story of a Kenyan whistle-blower.* San Francisco: Harper.

Yunus, Muhammad. 1999. *Banker to the poor: Micro-lending and the battle against world poverty.* New York: Public Affairs.

Zdero, Rad. 2004. *The global house church movement.* Pasadena: William Carey Library.

# INDEX

# SCRIPTURE INDEX